CHURRASCO

CHURRASCO

GRILLING THE BRAZILIAN WAY

EVANDRO CAREGNATO

Culinary Director of **Texas de Brazil**

Photographs by **Denny Culbert**

GIBBS SMITH
TO ENRICH AND INSPIRE HUMANKIND

20 19 18 17 16   5 4 3 2 1

Text © 2016 by Evandro Caregnato
Photographs © 2016 by Denny Culbert, except:
pages 6–7, 22–23, 34, 43–48, 203 and 205 © 2016 by Texas de Brazil
pages 4–5 and 24–31 © 2016 by Eurico Salis

Published by
Gibbs Smith
P.O. Box 667
Layton, Utah 84041
1.800.835.4993 orders
www.gibbs-smith.com

Design by Sheryl Dickert
Page production by Renee Bond
Food styling by Evandro Caregnato

Printed and bound in Hong Kong
Gibbs Smith books are printed on either recycled, 100% post-consumer waste, FSC-certified papers or on paper produced from sustainable PEFC-certified forest/controlled wood source. Learn more at www.pefc.org.

Library of Congress Cataloging-in-Publication Data

Caregnato, Evandro, author.
  Churrasco : grilling the Brazilian way / Evandro Caregnato ; Photographs by Denny Culbert. — First edition.
    pages cm
  ISBN 978-1-4236-4068-4
1. Cooking, Brazilian. 2. Barbecuing—Brazil. 3. Cooking—Texas.
I Title.
  TX840.B3C328 2016
  641.5981—dc23
                    2015029648

I dedicate this book to all past and present employees of the Texas de Brazil family. The effort, dedication, and passion of each one of them, regardless of title or occupation, are the ultimate reasons for our continued success. These ladies and gentlemen always give their very best while working long, late, and sometimes exhausting hours, frequently sacrificing precious family time to work during major holidays (and always with a smile) so that our guests and their families can enjoy a memorable time with us.

On a more personal level, this is for my lovely wife, Vanderleia (Dede); my daughter, Sophia; and my son, Lucca, who, like me, at the age of eight learned just how tasty churrasco can be and can no longer live without it.

The first Texas de Brazil location, opened in October 1998, Addison, Texas.

Contents

FOREWORD

When I experienced a churrascaria for the very first time, I was captivated by the savory aromas of grilled meats, the delectable array of side dishes, and the warm, casual atmosphere of people engaged in conversation over this regional Brazilian comfort food. The service style was alive and theatrical, unlike anything else in the restaurant business at that time. I found myself in awe and fell completely in love with the concept. Living in Dallas, I could immediately see the connection between the two cultures—the Brazilian gauchos and the Texas cowboys—and their shared reverence towards meat. Having worked in the hospitality industry for many years, I knew that very moment that this dining experience would appeal to BBQ lovers, especially in Texas.

However, opening such a unique restaurant was not easy and not without immense risk. It took a great deal of effort and sacrifice to go from conception to execution, but I was undaunted. Eventually, after many years of research, planning, and challenges, the first Texas de Brazil opened its doors in 1998.

I never imagined that the restaurant would expand, not only to more locations in the Dallas area, but also around the world. I am proud to say that what started as a family business, remains a family business to this day. And our "family" has expanded across the US and abroad through the efforts and collective passion of an amazing team of gifted "ladies and gentlemen"— namely, our honest, dedicated, and hardworking staff—whose outstanding commitment to service results in customer satisfaction and loyalty.

All of us at Texas de Brazil are committed to serving great churrasco and providing guests with a memorable dining experience. We are also committed to preparing and serving authentic churrasco in a manner that honors the rustic gaucho tradition. It is our hope that through this cookbook—written with great passion by our culinary director and native gaucho, Evandro Caregnato—our diners and any grilling aficionado will learn more about the origins and techniques of churrasco and then create and share this hearty and delicious cuisine with others.

—Salim Asrawi
COO, Texas de Brazil

FROM BRAZIL TO TEXAS DE BRAZIL

My Culinary Journey in the World of Churrasco

When I was a child growing up in southern Brazil, I was a picky eater and would not eat any meat. One day that all changed. I still remember that turning point: I was eight years old, it was a sunny, cloudless Sunday, and I was watching my father, Davino, grill skewers of meat. He pressured me into tasting some of the *churrasco* that he was preparing and cut a small piece of beef from the skewer—it was perfectly charred, glistening from the golden and slightly crispy fat that had been rendered in the wood fire. The look and smell enticed me to take a bite, and when the meat hit my lips, it was salty, juicy, and delicious. That one bite was pure perfection. My dad watched with great satisfaction because he knew— as did I—that I had reached an important milestone for a gaucho boy: I had officially become a carnivore!

I am frequently asked where I studied cooking, but there is no formal education for churrasco. My culinary experience is divided into two areas: churrasco and everything else. I have been cooking churrasco since my initiation in the backyard that Sunday afternoon. These skills were passed down to me during childhood, as they are for most young boys in Rio Grande do Sul. You learn from a father, grandfather, uncle, or any other paternal figure in your life. (Sorry, gaucho women, but in the gaucho culture men are considered the experts in grilling meat.)

I experienced this food culture firsthand and grew up wanting to emulate those older guys standing around the *churrasqueira*, drinking beer or caipirinhas and telling dirty jokes. Those moments around the grill were a rite of passage, and eventually, I wanted to prepare the churrasco for all of my family and friends and have control over the whole thing—the fire, the knives, the

seasoning of the meat, and the slow grilling to perfection. Like most teenagers in my culture, I was overconfident and wanted to show that I was ready for the experience. I overcooked the meat many times and frequently burned myself. Then, one day, I finally served a perfect churrasco and made my family proud. That's how I learned to love and master the art of churrasco.

As for the other part of my culinary experience, it is important to note that people in southern Brazil are not very open-minded when it comes to trying unfamiliar foods or seasonings, so I was never exposed to a diverse range of culinary options. Although I lived in a macho world of churrasco, charcoal, coarse salt, skewers, meat marinades, and fire, I loved being in the kitchen with the women in my family. My mother, Leda, and my aunts were always cooking something—making jams with seasonal fruits, baking bread in a backyard oven, or creating pastries and savories for the kids' birthday parties. The women had their own culinary traditions that were passed down by their mothers and grandmothers, which, in turn, they shared with their daughters and granddaughters (though I learned a thing or two as well). My mother and her sisters were always close, and they would get together several times a week to cook. As a kid, I felt warm and happy being around to help out in a kitchen filled with food and laughter.

I think the turning point in my culinary life was when my parents bought a microwave oven. Really—a microwave! My family was one of the first in my town to have one. Microwaves were so expensive that it was a sign of status to own one. The manufacturer, Sanyo, as I still remember clearly, hired a team of chefs to go from town to town to show the few privileged buyers how to operate the microwave and to demonstrate a few recipes. My mom took me along for the daily classes, which were held at the appliance store where she purchased the oven. Oddly enough, I was not only the only kid there, but I was also the only male. Even though I was just an observer, I loved it. That week of classes opened a new world for me. The chefs talked about techniques, discussed recipes and spices, demonstrated their knife skills, and created tasty dishes. (Fortunately, none of my friends found out about my sitting in on these classes or my budding interest in cooking; I probably would have been bullied extensively.)

When the classes ended, I started to think about food all the time and began using the microwave for everything. But when I realized that the food I was cooking was not better, just faster, I decided to experiment with new recipes using the regular oven and stove. Whenever I had spare time, I would cook almost every recipe from whatever books I could find. One of the first challenging recipes I tackled was a roasted whole leg of pork, marinated for several hours in Coca-Cola. The soda was supposed to transform into a rich syrup that would make a delicious glaze, but it didn't turn out well. I was very disappointed with the results, and my father was mad at me for wasting money on a cut of meat that I turned into something inedible. However, I was not deterred by the experience. Instead, I continued to experiment in the kitchen, and my self-taught cooking skills eventually improved.

When I completed my required school studies, I went to the university to study computer science. I didn't like it very much, and after two years, I switched my major to business administration. By the age of nineteen, I was eager to start making money, and I wanted to open a business—any business. After some thought, I decided to open a restaurant. But I didn't have the money, and my father didn't want to fund me (wise man). So I decided to start something on a smaller scale: I rented a large garage from my aunt Jandira and bought some used kitchen equipment, a freezer, and a refrigerator.

There were numerous manufacturing companies in town, many of which had no on-site food services, so I decided to focus my business on providing meals to their employees. Once I had the equipment, a van, and the space, I composed and printed a letter offering my services, pretending that my company had been in business for many years. I found the addresses of some medium-sized companies in the Yellow Pages and mailed a copy of the letter to each one. Three days later, I started getting calls from companies inquiring about my services. Unfortunately, some of them would ask for references or wanted to visit the kitchen, but since the kitchen was not functional yet, I reached a dead end. But I was lucky enough that one company only asked me how much I would charge to serve lunch to about seventy employees. I gave the cost and was asked if I could start on Monday. Of course, I said yes. That same day, I picked up my thirteen-year-old cousin, Daian Longhi, and drove fifty miles to buy a cow and cart back the meat in the back seat of my van. Since money was short, I offered my self and my cousin to help slaughtering and butchering the meat in exchange of small discount. Not the nicest experience.

We got home very late that night, much later than we expected, and Daian's parents were furious because we didn't inform them of our whereabouts. My aunt almost had a heart attack when she saw her son, his clothes splattered with blood. My cousin was grounded and forbidden to talk to me for almost a month. To this day, we still laugh about that incident, wondering how we mustered the courage to do it. Years later, Daian would come with me to the United States to help with the opening of Texas de Brazil.

I still remember the menu for the first lunch I provided for my new client, a relatively upscale clothing company: pumpkin ravioli, churrasco steak (from the meat I had butchered the day before), green bean casserole, rice, beans, a few different salads, and a very simple dessert. They loved it and I was in business! I began getting phone calls for my catering services from other companies, and since I could provide references, I signed up a few more clients. Soon, I was cooking for about 300 people a day; I bought another van and hired my first employees.

Those were hard working times—I was making a lot of money for my age but putting in about seventeen hours a day, seven days a week. On the weekends, when everyone else was going out and having fun, I would spend my Sunday afternoons making insane amounts of homemade pasta

for Monday's lunch service with my fiancée, Vanderleia Mallmann, who a few years later became my wife. We used a Torchio pasta extruder that I borrowed from my grandma—it's a manual pasta machine made of bronze that's used in some areas of northern Italy. I brought this pasta extruder to Texas a few years ago; I keep it to remind me to always be humble and that hard work and dedication pay off.

Before long, I moved my catering kitchen to a much larger space, bought a few more VW vans, and hired more cooks and drivers. Within three years, I was serving about 3,000 meals a day and making a good living. Although I had the chance to improve my cooking skills tremendously due to the high volume, the meals were nothing special or fancy. My customers didn't want anything different, and I started feeling bored.

All the meals needed to have 200 grams of protein, about 5.3 ounces of beef, pork, chicken, lamb, or sausage. To please my customers, half the time the meat would be cooked using the huge charcoal rotisserie that I had custom built for the catering business. I soon noticed that I was especially happy and less stressed on the days that I worked on the grill, turning skewers and smelling the smoke, just as I had as a boy. I realized that that was what I wanted to do—I wanted to cook churrasco full time. I wanted to have a *churrascaria*—not in my hometown or even in Brazil, but in Canada or the United States. I thought that people in other parts of the world should have a chance to experience churrasco in a real churrascaria. I didn't care whether or not I would make money, I just wanted to work at something that would bring me happiness and fulfillment. I told my wife about my dream and she supported me, probably thinking that I would forget the idea in a few days. But that same week, I visited my friend Tomasi, who manufactured the churrasco rotisserie that I was using, to ask what he knew about doing business in North America. It turned out he had exported rotisseries to some Brazilians and Americans in the United States who tried to open small churrascarias, but none of them succeeded. Tomasi gave me some advice and explained that it was not going to be easy. I left there feeling a little less enthusiastic and optimistic, but I was still motivated. I somehow believed that everything would work out and I would realize my dream.

Later that day, in a stroke of luck, Tomasi called to tell me that a businessman from Texas was coming by to purchase a rotisserie for a restaurant he was planning to open in Dallas. That man turned out to be Salah Izzedin, one of the future owners of Texas de Brazil. Tomasi asked if I would like to join them so that I could learn a little more about business in the United

States. A few hours later, I was in a room listening to the two of them trying to communicate using bits and pieces of Portuguese, Spanish, and English. At one point, Salah asked Tomasi who I was and what I was doing there. My friend told him about my business and background; he also mentioned that I was excited about someone opening a churrascaria in the United States and wanted to know more about the idea. The next thing I knew, Salah invited me to travel to Texas to work as a consultant.

At that time, I was a newlywed living in a comfortable house that my wife and I had built and loved. My wife and my parents didn't like the idea of my going to the United States for the consulting job, but I was very persuasive. We made a compromise—I would go to Texas for only three months to see if opening a churrascaria in the United States was feasible. I wanted to take my wife with me, but she could not leave her fashion and clothing business. I asked my cousin Daian to go with me instead. He initially didn't want to go—he was doing very well with his graphic design business and had little experience with churrasco aside from eating it—but it was a unique opportunity and a chance to see the United States and improve his English, so he accepted the challenge.

A few weeks later, the first Texas de Brazil opened in Addison, Texas, a northern suburb of Dallas. Preparing for the opening was busy and challenging. We had to work long, hard days, and sometimes I doubted we would make it. Eventually, our staff started to feel more comfortable with the style of service, and the meat servers got better and more skillful with the skewers and knives. Suddenly, I looked around and the whole thing felt right. Little by little, the restaurant got busier, and we could see many customers were excited to share this new dining experience with others, returning with friends and family in tow.

I also loved everything about Texas and its people—it felt like Rio Grande do Sul. Cowboys and gauchos share many common interests: horses, cattle, open fires, barbecue, and so much more. Like the cowboy, the gaucho's life was one of large ranches, vast grasslands that reached beyond the horizon, and a quasi-nomadic existence. Even today, the souls of our ancestors, whether cowboys or gauchos, still live within us. We are proud of our stubbornness, and we like to look tough and maintain our own style (whether it's boots and a cowboy hat or the *pilcha*). We both love and miss the simple life. For us, life is good when we have a campfire, a juicy steak, and a few good friends to share the experience. It was no wonder that I felt completely at home in Dallas and that I absolutely loved working with my new bosses. But my three-month contract

was about to expire, and I had tickets to return to Brazil just days before Christmas. I had already made some plans for my future, but I secretly knew I would be more than happy to continue with Texas de Brazil. There was only a single restaurant at that time, with little assurance that it would survive, but I had a gut feeling that something big was starting to happen. I wanted to be part of it.

Just days before the end of my consulting contract, I was called to Texas de Brazil's office and given the final check for my services. I thought that was it, but I was surprised to hear from my dear bosses, Salim and his mom Leila, that they wanted me to stay on and work for the company full time. Without hesitation, I went home to Caxias do Sul, sold my catering company, and returned to Texas—this time not with my cousin, but with my wife. That was March 1999, and the rest is history!

After almost two decades, we still keep the churrasco authentic at Texas de Brazil, cooking the meat the same way it has been done for many generations in my family. As I write this book, we are preparing to open our fortieth location and will be expanding aggressively in other parts of the world as no other churrascaria has done before. But it is not the numbers that make me proud. What makes me proud is that we didn't have to follow trends or study group behavior to achieve success. We believed that the most important thing to do was to stay close to our roots in Texan hospitality and traditional Brazilian food, and that is what the Texas de Brazil name represents.

I am very fortunate to work with people who respect the gaucho culture. I often tell our staff that we serve tradition. The gaucho churrasco is not something to be changed or modified to please different groups or trends. Instead, like tradition, churrasco is something to preserve, and Texas de Brazil understands and honors that.

With this book, I hope to do more than demonstrate how to cook at home some of the fantastic dishes we serve at Texas de Brazil and in southern Brazil. I want to introduce you to my culture and provide you with an orientation to gaucho history and traditions; then you will understand why we put so much love and respect into the food we cook for you.

GAUCHO CULTURE AND CUISINE

Tell me what you eat, and I will tell you who you are.
—JEAN ANTHELME BRILLAT-SAVARIN

When you see or hear the word "gaucho," your mind probably conjures up the image of a cowboy riding his horse along the Pampas of Argentina or Uruguay. Many people are unaware that there are gauchos in southern Brazil too, even though the Pampas region extends into the country. There have been times when Argentinian and Uruguayan guests have visited a Texas de Brazil location and felt confused or even offended, thinking we have borrowed and capitalized on their culture and heritage. When I explain that even though I am Brazilian, I am also a gaucho who wears the *pilcha*, drinks *chimarrão,* and enjoys *matambre*, they not only realize that the gauchos from our respective countries are the same, but we also become friends, bonded by a common culture.

There is a global perception that Brazil is a country of beaches with beautiful tan women, Carnival, the Amazon rainforest, the samba, and caipirinhas. While it's true that Brazil is home to all of these wonderful things, the gaucho way of life is a distinctive and integral part of the culture. In fact, rather than being called "Brazilian," most natives of the state of Rio Grande do Sul prefer to call themselves "gaucho," regardless of lifestyle, heritage, or the knack for mastering the art of churrasco. The gauchos have their own national anthem, long-established customs, traditional costumes, and food culture. When someone calls himself a gaucho, it's more than just a regional tie—it's also a state of mind, a declaration of cultural pride and values. This doesn't mean that gauchos don't feel like Brazilians—quite the opposite. We love being Brazilians and part of this vast, diverse, and beautiful country. But there is one thing every gaucho knows in his heart for sure: there is no better food than churrasco, and no one makes churrasco better than a gaucho.

A Brief History of Gauchos

When the first European explorers from Spain and Portugal arrived in South America in the fifteenth century, there were no gauchos; the native inhabitants in the Pampas were indigenous tribes like the Charrúa and Minuano, most of which perished at the hands of their conquerors. The few that remained were converted to Catholicism by the Jesuits (who established missions in the region) and subsequently intermarried with the Spaniards. These Mestiços were not recognized by their Spaniard fathers and were looked down on by the Indians. This marginalized and rugged group of people became known as gauchos; the Pampas became their home.

The early gauchos were a brave, nomadic people with few or no boundaries and without a government to serve or laws to observe. There were no chiefs or leaders; they were free to do whatever they wished and had no fear of consequences. Spending most of their time on horses, they survived on what little the land had to offer. Life was harsh, and most of them lived in

complete solitude, many in poverty and marginalized by society. Though they had roots in both indigenous and European cultures, they felt no true connection to either heritage. Not feeling a part of any culture or country, they forged their own culture and customs. Many eventually became ranchers or landowners, but they maintained their traditions and strong, rugged character, which was not unlike the legendary cowboys of the North American West.

In the mid-1800s, Rio Grande do Sul (which means "Great River of the South") attracted a large influx of German and Italian immigrants (like my grandparents, who came from Italy) looking to escape economic hardship and political instability. They were offered land in various regions of the state, particularly in the Região Serrana mountain region. These regions were mostly unpopulated, but the land and climate were suitable to the skills the Europeans possessed in farming, ranching, and even grape growing and winemaking. Many developed an existence based on agriculture and hunting.

Initially, the contact between the Europeans and gauchos was minimal. Over time, however, an interesting assimilation occurred: the Europeans, presumably

a more developed culture, began adopting many of the traditions and customs of the gauchos. Blue-eyed Germans began drinking chimarrão; Italians would dress as gauchos for traditional *bailes* (dance events); they incorporated words from the gaucho vocabulary into their own; and above all, they embraced the authentic culinary tradition of the gauchos—churrasco—as their most celebrated food. Unlike the New World explorers of centuries past, these European immigrants did not impose their culture on the natives; instead, they embraced the simple life of the gauchos. They looked upon these carefree people with a degree of envy, admiring their courage, strength, determination, and character. Hence, regardless of origin, they all became gauchos.

Today, gauchos like to see themselves as hardworking people with character and traditions that are very different from those of other Brazilians. Gauchos, even the younger generation, continue to maintain their customs and have their own music, dance, clothing, and dialect. Many gauchos still wear the pilcha—the traditional and distinctive attire comprised of wide, baggy trousers (called bombacha), a flat-brimmed hat with a chinstrap, a poncho, a fabric sash (tirador), a belt (guaiaca), a red neckerchief, and tall boots—daily. On holidays, families still dress in traditional costumes. One such celebration is Gaucho Day, on September 20, which commemorates a gaucho-led rebellion to make Rio Grande do Sul a separate country. Though the rebellion was defeated, the holiday celebrates the courage and bravery of the gauchos with an array of festivities, beginning with a parade of gauchos on horseback, followed by shows, rodeos, music, dance, and of course, churrasco.

The Origins of Gaucho Cuisine and Churrasco

"Cuisine" is probably too fancy a term to describe gaucho-style cooking. In the early days, and to some extent today, gauchos lived off the land and the animals they raised and eventually ranched, so their diet consisted mostly of beef. But beef was not native to Brazil. During the seventeenth and eighteenth centuries, the Jesuits came to the southern areas of South America (Uruguay, Argentina, and Paraguay) to establish reductions (settlements) in order to convert the indigenous tribes, the Charrúa and the Minuano, to Christianity. With them, they brought the first cows and horses, which until that time were nonexistent in South America. These reductions flourished, but they were under frequent attack from Portuguese soldiers and threatened by the assaults of *bandeirantes*—fortune hunters from the São Paulo area of Brazil—who were trying to capture the indigenous inhabitants to turn them into slaves for the sugar cane plantations farther north. Eventually, the reductions were destroyed and abandoned, the Jesuits left, and the surviving native tribes fled, returning to a nomadic lifestyle. Some of the cows and horses survived the destruction of the wars and turned wild. Over time, they reproduced to astonishing numbers due to the lack of predators, the mild weather, and the richness of the Pampas (which became one of the world's prime cattle regions). The natives that remained in the Pampas became excellent horse-riders, so meat from the wild herds of cattle was easy to obtain. Roasted meat was not just delicious, it was usually the only source of food. Historians say that it was common to kill an animal just for a quick snack and leave most of the carcass intact on the ground since meat was abundant and there was no need to preserve it for later.

As animals grazed freely on the Pampas, many impoverished gauchos realized that they could make money moving and selling cattle to distant and more populated areas, and so they soon capitalized on this. During these extremely long journeys, roasted meat was again the most accessible and satisfying food. The gauchos created their own style of cooking, which started with digging large ditches in the ground in which to make a fire from wood gathered around the camp. They would then select livestock from the herd, butcher it in a matter of minutes, and roast it slowly above the fire on skewers. The deep ditches kept the flames hot and protected against the harsh wind of the Pampas. The cooking process would last for hours, and the technique resulted in tender and succulent meat. When the cooking was complete, the

gauchos would cut pieces of meat from the skewers using an *adaga*, a knife that hung from their belts. This communal method of grilling and consuming meat came to be called "churrasco," which is Portuguese for "barbecue."

More than just a technique, churrasco soon became a way of life, not just on the range but also among families and friends. Groups would gather to cook and share meals—the men grilling the meat, the women preparing accompaniments and the table—and these feasts became regular events. Even babies partake in the meal by consuming small pieces of bread dipped in the juice that drips from the skewers of the meat as it cooks—a true induction into a carnivorous lifestyle. With this type of initiation, it's no wonder this Sunday afternoon mealtime event is an integral part of a gaucho's life.

The concept of churrasco spread throughout the region and became an inherent part of gaucho culture and identity. Most importantly, it became associated with joy and camaraderie. If there was a large event to celebrate, the gauchos would not say how many guests were invited; instead, they would brag about how many cows they would be slaughtering—this would give an idea of how big the event was going to be. Churrasco became synonymous with good times, family reunions, and celebrations.

In addition to churrasco, another gaucho staple is chimarrão (or yerba mate), a strong, caffeine-rich, tea-like beverage made from the leaves of the yerba tree. It is usually prepared and served in a gourd (*cuia*) and sipped through a metal straw (called a *bomba*). It is often shared among a group of people and passed around until the very last drop is consumed; the round is complete when a loud sucking sound is heard. Chimarrão is believed to have digestive qualities that prove helpful after eating a hearty meal of grilled meat. For gauchos, offering and sharing chimarrão is a symbol of acceptance, unity, and hospitality among family members or between friends.

Brazilian Cuisine: Beyond Churrasco

To many, particularly those outside South America, churrasco has become synonymous with Brazilian cuisine. It is not, however, the most popular food in Brazil. In fact, people in many parts of the country weren't familiar with it until a few years ago, when churrascarias started opening across the country and around the world.

Brazilian food, much like American food, is influenced by many cultures, but the most prominent influences are Brazil's indigenous tribes, the Portuguese, and Africans (the slave trade brought millions of Africans to the country, along with their unique food culture). A large wave of immigrants during the nineteenth and twentieth centuries brought additional diversity to Brazilian cuisine, with influences from Germany, Italy, Lebanon, Syria, and Ukraine.

If I had to pick what is considered the national dish of Brazil, I'd have to say *feijoada*, a bean and pork stew. Another food that is common throughout the country is *mandioca* (manioc), the root of the cassava plant, more familiarly known as yucca. Toasted manioc meal, called *farofa*, is a food staple; part side dish and part condiment, it is to Brazil what rice is to Asia. Brazilians all over the country also enjoy *salgadinhos*, savory snacks that are similar to tapas; they are popular at parties or as a quick bite during working hours. Some of these snacks include *coxinha*, a chicken croquette shaped like a drumstick, and *pastéis*, filled pastries similar to empanadas.

While churrasco is unique to Rio Grande do Sul, other regions and states of the country have their own popular dishes. In Bahia, a state located on the north coast of the country with a strong African influence and fresh seafood, there are *moqueca de peixe*, a coconut fish stew, and *acarajé*, falafel-like fried balls of black-eyed peas and onions. And in Minas Gerais, a state north of São Paulo and Rio de Janeiro, there's *pão de queijo*, which is a delicious cheese bread, as well as many pork dishes. Owing to the influence of Italian immigrants in Rio Grande do Sul, polenta and pasta round out meals in the south of the country. Brazilian cuisine is as diverse as its culture and its people, and many of these popular dishes are now found on the menu at churrascarias.

THE CHURRASCARIA EXPERIENCE

It is only natural that churrasco grew beyond the traditional gaucho experience on the Pampas. It spread to their families back home, then on to local gatherings, and eventually to the community at large in the form of roadside grilling and restaurants. That's how the churrascaria emerged.

A churrascaria is a restaurant that prepares authentic gaucho-inspired barbecue consisting of various cuts of freshly cooked meats served hot off the grill on skewers. Several servers (also called *passadores* or gauchos) make the rounds, each with a different type of meat. Beef is the main feature, but other options include lamb, pork, and chicken. The meat is carved tableside to the customer's preference, allowing him or her to choose the type of meat and the level of doneness, which provides an interactive dining experience. This serving style is called *rodizio*. Many churrascarias supply customers with green and red cards or wooden blocks so that servers can see which customers would like more food (green) and which ones are currently satisfied (red).

While grilled meats are the stars of this dining show, the experience also includes side dishes that are brought to the table and a separate salad area featuring various appetizers, soups, and salads to round out the meal. (When outside of southern Brazil, it seems that man cannot survive on meat alone!) The salad area also provides an alternative for those in a dining group who may not be as carnivorous or who have smaller appetites. At most churrascarias, dining is done as a prix fixe (fixed price) meal, inclusive of the meats, side dishes, and salad area selections or just the salad area alone. Beverages and desserts are usually charged separately.

While many churrascarias stay close to their traditional roots, others have become more "modern." Some have a huge sushi station; some have chefs with pots of exotic fresh risottos visiting each table; some even serve pizza tableside. But the best and most authentic churrascarias are those that focus on the meat—everything else should merely complement the good steak.

Differences between Churrascarias and Other Steakhouses

The gauchos from Argentina, Uruguay, and Rio Grande do Sul have a lot in common. Their cultures and traditions are very similar; for example, they all love the yerba mate, and they all love to cook and eat large amounts of meat— the assado. But you may be surprised to learn that the term "churrascaria" is unknown in Argentina and Uruguay; this term is exclusively from southern Brazil, more specifically my home state of Rio Grande do Sul. Gauchos from these three countries all cook meat over open flames with very few seasonings or spices, usually just coarse salt. In Brazil, we call it *churrasco*; in Argentina and Uruguay, it's called *parrillada*. The cooking techniques, however, are slightly different.

Traditional steakhouses in Argentina cook their meats "parrilla-style," where the meat cooks over burning wood or charcoal on a flat metal grate and an *asador* turns the cuts using a long pair of tongs. The Brazilian gauchos don't use this system; instead, they pierce the large pieces of meat with long metal skewers and cook the meat over the burning charcoal, turning the skewers by hand until done. But the most significant difference between these two steakhouses is the service. In Argentina, and in Argentinian steakhouses, you order a steak from a menu and have it delivered to your table, but in a Brazilian steakhouse, you are served tableside by passadores and get to sample all the cuts offered for a single price. Additionally, Brazilian steakhouses offer a salad area with different salads, soups, sides, and charcuteries as part of the fixed price. In Argentinian steakhouses, salads and sides are ordered separately, much like in an American steakhouse.

The First Churrascarias

Though churrasco has been around for centuries, the churrascaria is a more recent concept. During the mid-twentieth century, when the construction of roads began connecting small towns in Brazil, general stores and gas stations opened up. Some of these business owners decided to add a table or two to serve food to truck drivers and other hungry travelers, and grilled meat was one of the easiest and cheapest foods to serve, as well as being a mainstay of the gaucho diet. These roadside venues would cook large pieces of meat on skewers over

an open flame and sell each skewer separately. There were no rotisseries back then, so the meat was usually cooked outdoors in tin-roofed, wall-less rooms. The charcoal would burn on the ground, and a few bricks would support the skewers, which were then made out of wooden spears. There was no menu and patrons would be served whatever type of beef was available, usually cooked well done since the meat would be sitting over the heat for hours. Back then, the meat was not carved tableside. Often, the grill master (usually the owner or one of his sons) would place the skewer of beef on the table and leave; other times, a large construction brick with holes would be used as a base to keep the skewer standing straight, allowing the guests to carve chunks of meat and eat to their hearts' content. As these roadside food venues gained popularity, more tables were added, and regardless of the rustic and simple menus, they soon looked more like restaurants than gas stations and stores.

It is almost impossible to determine which restaurant introduced the rodizio (rotation or "skewer run") service. There are many restaurants in Brazil claiming the title of the first churrascaria in the world, so we may never know

for sure. But in Rio Grande do Sul, this distinction belongs to a place called Churrascaria Matias, not far from my home in Caxias do Sul. Rumor has it that in the 1960s, this restaurant slow roasted not only beef but also pork, lamb, chicken, and sausage. The style of service was still the same, but the guests could order a whole skewer of a single cut of meat and pay accordingly. If you wanted to sample beef and lamb, you would have to order two skewers and pay for each one, regardless of how much you or your party could eat, but you could take home any leftovers. The concept remained unchanged for many years, until one day, with a full house, one of the servers mistakenly delivered skewers of meat to the wrong table. The guest took it upon himself to sample the meat, which was to his liking. Though it broke the house rules, the server rested the skewer on the table and let this guest take a little piece of the roast with his knife, hoping that the owner and other patrons were not paying attention. A nearby guest witnessed what had happened and also asked to sample the meat. The server couldn't provide a good reason to decline this request, so he let this guest sample the meat too. Suddenly, everyone was asking to sample *all* the cuts, creating a gastronomic frenzy. The owner astutely realized a novel idea had just been born, so he walked to the middle of the small dining room and asked the guests if they would consider paying a single price to sample all the cuts served that night—as much as they wanted—on the condition that they could not take home any unfinished portions. Everyone agreed and the first rodizio-style restaurant in Rio Grande do Sul (and quite possibly Brazil) was created.

The rodizio system became very popular, and almost instantly, many other restaurants serving churrasco adopted this new style. Competition got tougher and restaurant owners added new meat options in an effort to steal customers from their rivals. That explains why churrascarias today offer such a wide variety of meat and poultry options—everything from chicken hearts to beef tenderloin, lamb chops, and pork ribs. Some cuts, like *picanha*, became instant classics, while others, like pig liver, were quickly discontinued.

Most early churrascarias didn't have a salad area like they do today. Simple salads were brought to your table, usually lettuce with red wine vinegar and oil and potato salad, along with a few rustic dinner rolls baked in-house. When these restaurants had exhausted new meat options to offer, they began adding more salads, sides, and even soup in order to attract and retain clientele. Eventually, the guest tables were not big enough to accommodate all these accompaniments, so a creative restaurant owner decided to set up a dedicated table for these items. With the big table, even more dishes could be offered, and a wood-burning stove was set nearby so that guests could serve themselves hot items like rice, beans, and potatoes. The introduction of the bountiful salad area forever changed the way gauchos ate—and the modern churrascaria was born.

Since the 1960s, many gauchos have left Rio Grande do Sul for employment opportunities in other areas of Brazil, moving north and west to states like Santa Catarina, Paraná, São Paulo, Goiás, and Mato Grosso. Many of these gauchos opened churrascarias, and being proud of their origins, they would wear the traditional gaucho outfit while they worked. In fact, at most churrascarias today, the meat servers still wear the same outfit. People from

other parts of Brazil loved this unique concept, so it became very popular. To keep up with demand, churrascaria owners would invite their brothers, cousins, and other relatives to come help them. Business was so good that once these family members could save enough money, they would leave to open their own churrascarias. The new churrascaria owners would then repeat the process of bringing their family members to work for them. Because the churrascaria owners were usually from rural areas of Rio Grande do Sul, this cycle had an effect on population. In fact, the town of Nova Bréscia lost most of its inhabitants to churrascarias in other parts of the country. If you visit a churrascaria in any large city in Brazil, there is a good chance that the owner and many of the staff can trace their roots back to Nova Bréscia. I am proud to say that my family has ties to this town too. Today, Nova Bréscia is the unofficial capital of churrasco—there is even a large statue of a *churrasqueiro* holding a skewer in the main plaza.

A Feast for All Palates

It is hard to deny that people from every corner of the world love beef cooked over an open flame with that smoke-kissed flavor. However, we all like a bit of variety. If you dine at a traditional American steakhouse, you may get a fantastic, perfectly cooked rib-eye or tenderloin. The first bite will be amazing, and so will the second, but when you are halfway through, the amazing taste of the steak becomes a little boring. You may start to wonder if you should have ordered something else, so you look at the plate of the person next to you and see gorgeous lamb chops—suddenly you are struck with "order regret syndrome." When you dine at a churrascaria, you don't have this problem. You don't have to worry about what to order because you can sample as many cuts as you desire. After you savor a tender and juicy piece of filet mignon, a different server will stop by with perfectly charred lamb chops. Minutes later, you find yourself with a slice of picanha and a sausage. Later, when you decide to give the pork loin a try, you think, "This pork is so good, but I would never have ordered it if I had to pick a single cut." That is the beauty and bounty of a churrascaria: After sampling a wide variety of meats, some familiar and some not, you can select the options to suit your mood and palate that night and enjoy them to the fullest. And because churrascarias do not use any exotic seasoning or spices other than salt, it is easy to please everyone's tastes.

In addition to a delicious range of dishes, churrascarias can also offer convenience. Whether you need to catch a seven thirty movie or a nine o'clock concert, you can be served promptly and control the pace of your meal to accommodate your schedule when you are pressed for time. You can even make a run to the salad area to select your accompaniments and be back to the table in time for the next gaucho's skewer without missing a beat.

Getting the Best Dining Experience at a Churrascaria

When you are planning to dine at a churrascaria, the best advice I can give is to come hungry! If visiting for the first time, you will want to try everything—every type of meat, every salad, and every side dish. This ensures a complete experience. On your next visit, you will know exactly what you like and will have saved your appetite to indulge in the meal fully. Many first-timers think that they will eat nothing but tenderloin, but once they try the picanha, they realize why it is the favorite cut in Brazil. Some of our restaurant regulars have one item they solely indulge in, such as lobster bisque or lamb chops. We even have one guest who only eats sausage with a bottle of

expensive Cabernet, to the exclusion of anything else. He says that the combination of our grilled sausage and the Cabernet is pure perfection and that he doesn't want to spoil the experience.

If you like cocktails before dinner, try a caipirinha before you start eating. This is the signature cocktail of Brazil, and it is refreshing and satisfying. Not only will you become more relaxed to enjoy the experience, but it will also increase your appetite.

Next, pay a visit to the salad bar, which is wonderfully abundant. I highly recommend enjoying a small bowl of lobster bisque along with the cheese bread. When you return for a second round, you might do what I do—create an antipasto platter from some of the other fresh selections. All Texas de Brazil restaurants offer a wonderful Manchego cheese from Spain and a fantastic smoked ham called speck, similar to prosciutto, from the Alto Adige region of Northern Italy. We also display a huge 80-pound wheel of Grana Padano cheese, so my antipasto platter will have these two types of cheeses,

the speck, some vinegary cornichons, and some slices of freshly baked bread that is especially good with a drizzle of olive oil. Before the meat course begins, get a clean plate and go back to the salad area for side dishes. Be sure to try the potato salad, because it is always served with churrasco in Brazil—it complements any meat perfectly.

As the servers make their rounds with skewered meats, you'll notice that some are served in pieces (like sausage, filet mignon with bacon, and lamb chops), while other meats are carved tableside. For the meats carved tableside, you'll use the set of tongs in your table setting; catch the slice of succulent meat as it is being carved and add it to your plate. (The tongs are easier to use than a fork for grabbing the meat.) Don't be nervous about having a carving knife so close to you—all servers at churrascarias are properly trained.

Most cuts of beef and lamb are prepared medium-rare to medium, with a few pieces leaning toward medium-well. If you request a specific preparation, the servers will do their best to accommodate you, so don't be shy about speaking up. It is interesting to note that Texas de Brazil doesn't have a designated grill master—the server carving the leg of lamb for you is also the one that cooked it. Each gaucho is assigned one cut of meat to cook and serve, allowing him to control the process from start to finish and inspiring a true sense of pride. Meats are delivered to the table in accordance with whatever is hot off the grill. However, I recommend holding off on pork ribs until the end of your meal because the barbecue sauce from the ribs can diminish the flavor of the other meats on your plate. I've even instructed our servers to wait until the guest is almost finished before serving pork ribs.

Many churrascarias routinely serve plates of fried bananas at the start of the meal. If they arrive at your table, you should try them between meat courses because they act as a palate cleanser. Take a small bite of these sugar-coated bananas, and then try a little piece of the slightly salty flap meat with golden fat bits—you'll find it heavenly.

Re-creating the Experience at Home: It's More Than Just Food

Believe it or not, the churrascaria is not only about food—dining companions are just as important. If you're thinking of creating a gaucho-style dinner or Sunday lunch, make it festive and invite as many friends and family members as you can. This type of experience is about the camaraderie of good friends and people who make you laugh.

Over the years, I've learned something valuable. For some time, the weekend churrascos that I attended or hosted back home in Brazil consisted of guests from the same age group. As a teenager, I thought that having a barbecue with my parents and grandparents wasn't cool or exciting. But I soon came to realize that the best churrasco dinners were those that included a variety of relatives of different ages, including grandma and grandpa, the cranky uncle, the mother-in-law, and even a crazy neighbor or two. They all brought life to the party with interesting conversations and many reasons to laugh, including a few pranks. The kids and babies that were once considered annoying actually rounded out the fun. You get the point: churrasco is special because it provides the perfect opportunity to gather the people you really care about and with whom you want to share time and good food.

Re-creating the full churrascaria experience at home can be a challenge. Sure, you could prepare a few salads, create a salad bar area, and then spend your time making the rounds and serving meat to your guests, but you would be depriving yourself of a good time. And honestly, the whole thing would be awkward.

Instead, you can re-create the whole *atmosphere* of a Sunday churrasco event like many Brazilians do. How? After you get your guest list together, start by thinking about these three must-have items: good music, smoke, and caipirinhas.

Imagine this: You are invited to a party, and when you arrive at the door, you can immediately smell the smoke and intoxicating aroma of meats grilling. You hear music in the background, and when you enter the house, the host greets you and hands you a caipirinha—how can this not lead to a great time?

For music, play whatever you like, but please do not play samba! Samba and churrasco don't go together, really. If you want something truly Brazilian, bossa nova is a great option because it is cool and jazzy although not gaucho. Even

música sertaneja could work. I personally would play some traditional gaucho music, but many would mistake it for Mexican country music. If you want a suggestion of something authentically gaucho, download a few songs from Oswaldir e Carlos Magrão. I have yet to meet a gaucho that doesn't like them.

The next ingredient is smoke. It immediately makes people hungry and happy. Perhaps it is because humans have been connected to fire since pre-historic times. The fire provided warmth, but the smoke was a sign that roasted meat would soon be served. It's a true mood-enhancer. One very old trick that is still used by many churrascarias in southern Brazil is to save all the fat trimmings from the butchered meats and throw them on the fire about an hour before service commences. If you happen to be walking or even driving by a churrascaria, you will not be able to resist the smell and may be lured inside to dine. You should definitely try the same technique at home. Save some fat trimmings and throw a few pieces on the grill when you are getting the charcoal ready. The fat will help to burn the charcoal, and the smell will be deliciously enticing. Speaking of charcoal, make sure to use natural hardwood charcoal; some chips of mesquite or pecan wood would help too (there will be more on charcoal in the next chapter).

And, finally, the caipirinha. Create a station with limes, perfectly ripe strawberries, pineapple, grapes, and kiwi, along with plenty of cachaça, simple syrup, and ice. Put someone in charge of making the caipirinhas for the guests, and make sure the cocktails are flowing—this is a surefire way to get everyone relaxed, engaged in conversation, and eating food. Believe me—the great food will taste even greater with caipirinhas. (The recipe for the classic caipirinha can be found on page 204.)

Another thing to consider for the churrasco atmosphere is making the event simple. Churrasco done in a family setting is unpretentious. It's fine to use disposable plates, and it's not necessary for everyone to be seated at the same time. Most gaucho families feed the young kids first and then let them go play while the adults sit down to eat.

Now that you have the atmosphere, let us discuss the food. To make the cooking truly authentic, consider making a churrasco grill from an oil drum (see page 81). I guarantee that it will draw the guests around it, and the return on your investment of time will be well worth the effort. Place a table next to the grill (any type of table will do) to hold the seasonings and the caipirinha glasses and beer bottles of the guests standing nearby.

As for the meats you'll be preparing, flap meat and picanha are essential, along with some sausages, chicken drumsticks, and chunks of pork loin. (If

you are really adventurous, add some chicken hearts too.) Recipes for all of these meats are included in later chapters.

Now that the charcoal is burning and the grill is ready, start by cooking the chicken, pork loin, and sausage. The pork loin should be the first meat to cook through. Cut the loin into pieces and toss them with fresh Parmesan. Pierce the pork loin pieces with some frilly toothpicks, and then walk around offering them to your guests. By this time, they will be standing around sipping caipirinhas, ready for a bite of something juicy and flavorful. When they try the first bite, they will love you.

A few minutes later, the sausages will be ready. Cut them into small pieces and serve them over a platter of farofa (toasted cassava flour). Your guests will devour them quickly and wonder what tasty surprise you'll have next.

Season the flap meat and picanha generously with salt and place the skewers over the flame. By this time the chicken will be ready, so transfer that to a platter and serve. When the beef is cooked, move it to the side of the grill to rest. Meanwhile, check to see that your salad table is set with a simple green salad, a few small bowls of chimichurri sauce (page 72) and campeiro salsa (page 154), and a basket of steaming cheese bread or freshly baked dinner rolls.

When the salad table is set and the meat is ready, grab one skewer each of flap meat and picanha, walk proudly to the table, place the meat on a large wooden cutting board (please do not use plastic), slide the meat off the skewers, and demonstrate your knife skills by slicing thin pieces of the meat. Guests can then serve themselves. It may be helpful to recruit a friend or to hire someone to help prepare and serve so that you are free to enjoy the food with your guests. Of course, they can also help with the cleanup later on.

This is how generations of gauchos have entertained their family and friends. For us, this is not a trend or something to be improved by later generations. Churrasco is part of our lives, and we are proud of it—so much so that many of us moved to other parts of the world to open churrascarias so that we could share the tradition with you. Now, you can share it with those you love.

CHURRASCO BASICS: MEAT, PREPARATION, AND GRILLING TECHNIQUES

As you probably know, practice makes perfect. That is why a gaucho's churrasco is so good, because gauchos have infinite chances to practice the technique. In southern Brazil, celebrations are just an excuse to make churrasco—and we celebrate a lot. Build yourself a simple grill, get some skewers, and play with fire. Practice the tips in this chapter, and soon you will be cooking like a gaucho.

The Two Key Churrasco Elements: Sal Grosso and Carvão (Salt and Fire)

There is no doubt that using high-quality meat is essential for a great churrasco, but there are two other important elements for successful Brazilian-style grilling: salt and fire. Churrascarias in Brazil generally use a little more salt than we use at Texas de Brazil. Gauchos like their churrasco seasoned heavily, as does the rest of the country. Brazilians dream about a thin slice of perfectly grilled picanha with *sal grosso*. Sal grosso is a very coarse salt, almost as coarse as the salt used to melt snow. In Brazil, all cooking salt is sea salt, the majority of which comes from the sunny areas of the Nordeste, where sea water from the Atlantic Ocean is pumped into large pools and left to evaporate naturally until only a thin crust of salt remains. The traditional salt for churrasco is minimally processed and is not completely white—it has a light silver, almost gray color. It is also inexpensive, which may be a reason why it is used so generously.

Most churrascarias in Brazil don't use salt shakers; instead, salt is poured into large pans. The churrasqueiro takes a handful of salt and covers the

meat completely with the coarse crystals, applying it loosely and generously but never rubbing it into the meat. When the meat is fully cooked, the grill master removes two skewers from the grill and, holding one in each hand, beats one skewer against the other a few times with relative force to release some of the excess salt. This process usually makes a mess on the floor, but it is the traditional way. (Old-time churrasqueiros would dust the floor with a bag of *farinha de mandioca* [cassava flour] to keep it from getting too slippery.)

Most Brazilians expect to find some visible pieces of salt on the thin slices of meat, as the salt provides a bit of crunch. When we opened the first Texas de Brazil back in Addison, Texas, we imported the traditional sal grosso from Brazil, but many guests complained about its texture, and we had to give assurances that the crystals on their plates were not tiny pieces of glass. So, I decided that we would need to use something else. We tried many different products, including the French *fleur de sel*, which gave the meat a slightly perfume-like essence, but none worked well. I finally discovered the product

that we still use, which I highly recommend: kosher salt. Diamond Crystal is our favorite brand of this flaky salt, and it can be found in most supermarkets. The granules are just the right size for the salt shakers at the restaurant and are less salty than other products.

The other key element is fire. By fire, I mean charcoal—*carvão* in Portuguese. While Argentinians and Uruguayans cook their assados (roasts) with wood, the Brazilian churrasco always uses charcoal. Charcoal is made by heating wood for days in a controlled environment, like a silo, without the presence of oxygen. Once the process is complete and the wood has cooled, the larger pieces are broken down and the charcoal is then bagged for sale. It comes as no surprise that the charcoal business is large and thriving in southern Brazil since families typically buy at least one bag of charcoal a week—and that is in addition to the charcoal purchased by restaurants.

Charcoal in Brazil is made from native trees, mostly acacia and eucalyptus wood. These semi-hard woods produce a good charcoal that burns hot for a long time with a good amount of smoke. It is important to understand that you should never let the flames touch the meat. Take the meat to the grill only when the charcoal is completely burned, glowing orange, and covered with a thin layer of white ash. This is when the magic happens: The embers will be so hot that in minutes the fat from the meat will start to melt and drip over the charcoal, creating an incredible white smoke that engulfs the meat. This smoke is fundamental to creating the characteristic flavor of churrasco.

As with the salt, we experimented with several different charcoals when we opened our first three locations. Mesquite charcoal, mostly from Mexico, is largely available and not expensive, but it created too many sparks (tiny pieces of floating charcoal) that stuck to the meat, making it look like the meat was covered with black pepper. These same sparks would also burn holes in our servers' shirts. Today we use South American charcoal made from natural hardwood that comes from renewable forests.

There are many excellent brands of charcoal for churrasco-style cooking, but we only use lump charcoal. We do not add any wood to the charcoal, but you can play around with it, maybe adding a few pieces of pecan or mesquite chips for an extra layer of flavor.

Traditional Churrasco Cuts

If you frequently dine at churrascarias, you've probably noticed that they all tend to serve the same cuts, whether in the United States, Brazil, or any other part of the world. Why? Because while there is not a single cut of beef, lamb, pork, or chicken that hasn't been fired up churrasco style, only a few work successfully. There are several criteria to consider. First, the cut must be able to be skewered and cooked over a flame. Second, because it will be served table to table around the dining room, it must retain its quality and freshness for a time after cooking. Third, it must be easy to carry and carve tableside; otherwise, it will slow down the service considerably and compromise the experience. Last, and most importantly, it has to be well accepted by the guests; if it is not, the guest will try it but then leave it on the plate, raising the food cost. Churrascarias consider all of these factors when choosing what meats to serve, and most restaurants now agree that the following cuts are the most favorable for this kind of cooking and easy carving.

Below are the types of meats and poultry to consider when preparing to cook churrasco at home, along with buying and grilling tips.

BEEF CUTS

Picanha

In many parts of the world, the tenderloin is prized as the king of the beef cuts, but in southern Brazil this award is reserved for the picanha. Picanha and churrascarias are indivisible. You cannot have a churrascaria without picanha, and the picanha gained its status and popularity by becoming the favorite cut served at churrascarias.

The origin of the name "picanha" is uncertain, but here's the explanation I like the most: Many years ago, in the Pampas between Brazil and Uruguay, where Spanish and Portuguese cultures and languages crossed, one gaucho was mesmerized by the taste of a piece of grilled meat. He asked the *parrillero* (grill master) what part of the animal he had eaten. The parrillero retorted with customary curtness, *"No sé. Es donde se pica la aña,"* or "It is where one brands the cow with the hot iron." *Pica la aña* eventually turned into *picanha.*

Though picanha did not originate with the gauchos, they were the first to develop the brilliant technique of folding the meat to create a cap and to skewer and roast it over an open flame. The cap of fat protects the meat during cooking, keeping it moist and juicy while creating a delicious crust that tastes like no other cut of beef.

In the United States, picanha is known as coulotte or sirloin cap. Cows have one on each side, located between the leg and end of the loin. (This cut is listed in *The Meat Buyer's Guide* with the code 184D. *The Meat Buyer's Guide* (MBG) is a catalog created by the North American Meat Institute [NAMI] that is intended for butchers, cooks, and commercial meat buyers. This guide is recognized as a reference for cutting and grading meat. The MBG maintains a standard numbering system for each cut of meat, so traders and chefs find it easier to call a certain cut by its number instead of its description. For example, instead of asking for a whole beef tenderloin, side muscle off and skinned, they would simply say "190A.") The picanha comes from the top sirloin and can be easily separated by hand from the whole sirloin butt. One side of the picanha will have the fat cap, averaging about 1 1/2 inches in thickness; the other side, which is attached to the sirloin, will have a silver skin and other connective tissues. The cap of fat should be trimmed to 1/2 inch, and the connective tissues on the other side should be completely removed and trimmed. The picanha resembles the tri-tip, as it has almost the

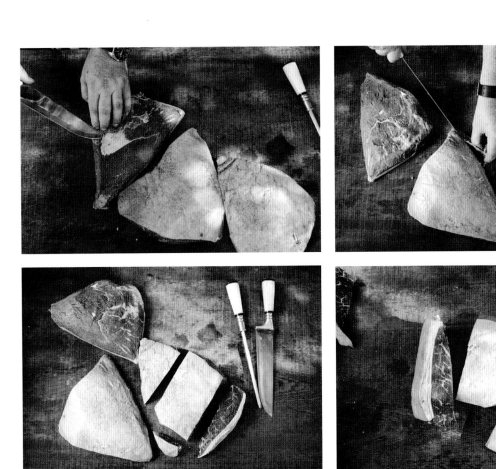

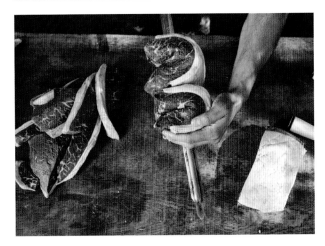

Preparing picanha for grill.

same size and a very similar shape, but the fat from the tri-tip is spongy, while the fat from the picanha is very firm, almost waxy. Both cuts look so similar that many Brazilians in the United States often think that tri-tip is the American name for picanha. In Brazil, the tri-tip is called *chapéu de bispo* (bishop's hat) by the gauchos and *maminha* by the rest of the country. Although maminha is a tasty cut and appreciated by many, it is the poor cousin of the picanha and very few churrascarias serve it.

It is almost impossible to find picanha at your local supermarket. You may have a better chance finding it in an independent butcher, especially at a *carnicería*, which is a butcher shop catering to and found in Latin neighborhoods. Since many carnicerías buy whole pieces of meat and disassemble the carcass, they should be able to detach the picanha from the sirloin and sell it to you. It will cost a little more than the top sirloin, but it's worth the expense.

A smaller picanha, weighing no more than 3 pounds (after the fat is trimmed) and with very white fat, is a good sign that the animal was young and fed well. Larger picanhas—or those with yellow fat—are signs of an older animal. Young animals will produce a more tender beef.

Like any other premium cut of beef, good marbling is desirable. We try to buy as much Prime-grade picanha for the restaurant as possible, but availability is extremely limited since only about 3 percent of the beef in the United States is graded as Prime.

I've also learned over the years that the terroir of the beef is as important as the grade. Terroir is the natural environment—climate, soil, and topography—that imparts a distinctive flavor to food items like wine, fruit, cheese, and meat. Given my well-trained palate for beef, I can readily distinguish the origins of the picanha I eat. There is a huge difference in flavor in picanha from South America, Australia, and North America. Beef from South America and Australia usually comes from cows that are grass fed for their entire life cycle; North American cattle roam freely in the pasture for most of their lives, but they are finished on grains for a few months before butchering. This is what, in my opinion, creates a sweeter flavor and more marbling, which results in tender beef. Our guests often ask where we obtain our meat: the majority of our beef comes from cattle raised in the Midwestern United States.

Given its importance to the churrascaria experience and its almost cult-like idolatry among gauchos, you will not find many recipes for picanha in this book. It is truly best when prepared in a simple manner that reveals its naturally beefy flavor.

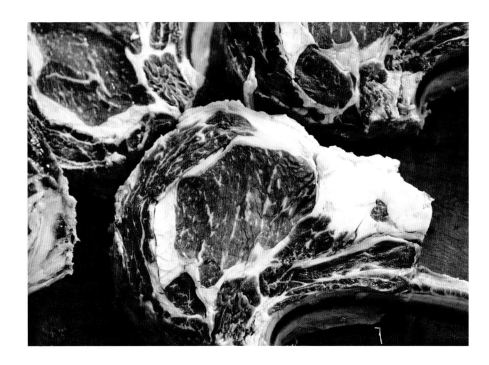

Flap Meat Steak

There is a lot of confusion surrounding the nomenclature of this cut. When guests at the restaurant see the flap meat that we serve on skewers, they often ask if it is skirt steak, hanger steak, or flank steak—but those are completely different cuts. Flap meat (185A) is larger and thicker than skirt or hanger steak. And if you place flank steak and flap meat side by side, you will notice the difference immediately—the flank steak has long fibers, while the fibers for the flap meat run sideways.

Because flap meat is much thicker, it maintains its juices while cooking. The flavor is also different from flank steak, which doesn't have the fat coverage to enhance its flavor and juiciness. Another difference is that flap meat derives from the bottom sirloin butt, very close to the picanha, while the flank steak is cut from the bottom of the short-loin portion of the steer.

Although very tasty, flap meat is a cut that needs to be aged a minimum of twenty-one days; otherwise, it will be very chewy. The grade is important too, so purchase meat that is USDA Choice or Prime whenever possible. When buying this cut, make sure the butcher doesn't completely remove the external fat. The external fat is as important as the internal marbling in this cut, and if you cook it completely stripped of fat, the fibers will dry out and harden.

Tenderloin/Filet Mignon

Beef tenderloin, also known as filet mignon, is the most expensive cut of beef, at least in the United States (filet mignon often refers to the end piece of the tenderloin). True to its name, it is very tender—this muscle doesn't work hard, which makes the fibers delicate. Surprisingly, given its expense, it is not the most flavorful cut of beef, which is why most steakhouses serve it with some kind of sauce or a large dollop of melted butter on top.

The tenderloin is a long muscle that runs along the spine of the cow. There is one on each side, so each animal produces two tenderloins. Not all churrascarias in Brazil serve it—only the most refined establishments—and most gauchos don't care much about it. It is not uncommon in southern Brazil to find this cut "on sale" at small local butchers.

Tenderloin is a temperamental cut of meat to cook using skewers—the meat turns gray and fibrous if overcooked—but many people still love it. At Texas de Brazil, we serve this cut two ways: petite tenderloins of about 3 ounces each, simply seasoned with salt and black pepper, and filet mignon with bacon, which is my favorite.

Buying tenderloin is easy, as it's readily available at most supermarkets, specialty stores, and butchers. Prime grade is best, Choice is excellent too, and Select is completely acceptable. As far as aging, tenderloin doesn't seem to benefit from the process as much as other cuts of beef. For flavor, I prefer the milder, sweeter grain-fed tenderloin to grass-fed. I would suggest that you purchase and prepare the grass-fed meat once and decide for yourself. You might even consider cooking grass-fed and grain-fed tenderloin side by side and comparing the taste.

When buying this cut, keep in mind that you will pay more for it when it is completely denuded of fat. If you have some butchering skills, you can undertake peeling away the fat and silver skin from the loin yourself.

On a side note, I had a piece of bull tenderloin in Europe a few years ago, and I didn't like it at all. It had a strong, gamey flavor and I could not take more than two bites. Thankfully, the vast majority of tenderloin in the United States comes from steers.

Beef Ribs

You may be surprised to know that at Texas de Brazil we don't mind using Select-grade short plate ribs with three bones (123A), rather than solely Choice or Prime grade. The other cuts of beef that we serve are cooked at a very high temperature to sear the juices in, and since we want a nice crust

with a medium to medium-rare center, the meat needs to be of Choice or Prime grade to achieve this. This doesn't apply to the short ribs, however; they are cooked slowly, for several hours, until they become tender. For this application, Select is sufficient and has more than enough intramuscular fat to keep the meat moist while it cooks.

In terms of flavor, grade and aging aren't a factor. Since the meat is cooked slowly and at length over the charcoal at a very low temperature, smoke becomes the key flavor element. While all other cuts of beef we use are always fresh and never previously frozen, the short ribs are, again, an exception. When shopping, if only frozen ribs are available and you cook it as we do, frozen is perfectly fine.

The final observation: If buying fresh ribs, smell the cut section of the bone. The material inside the bone tends to spoil much faster than the meat, so if it has a suspicious smell, do not buy it.

PORK CUTS

Pork Loin

The boneless loin of the pig is a juicy and tender cut, but it needs attention when cooking to avoid drying it out. It is a very affordable cut, and most of the available pork loins at your butcher shop should be satisfactory. I would not prepare this cut without an overnight marinade; it lacks flavor if too little seasoning is used. Pork loin is available two ways: center cut or with the chain attached. The chain is the meat and fat that is connected to the bones, and it's full of flavor. I always prefer it with the chain attached. Like most cuts of beef, you need some protective cap of fat to prevent the pork from drying out when cooking over an open flame.

Many people think that pork loin is the same cut as the beef tenderloin, but it is not; in fact, pork loin is the equivalent of the beef rib-eye and strip. Additionally, pork loin and pork tenderloin are different cuts—pork tenderloin would be equivalent to the beef tenderloin. Like the beef cut, the pork tenderloin is expensive but tender and significantly tastier.

Buying good pork is not as difficult as buying good beef—just make sure it is as organic and natural as possible. When I was growing up in Brazil, all the pork we ate at home came from a relative's ranch, where the animals were raised free range. In addition to eating grains, the pigs would forage for food. This diet is similar to that of wild boars and would ensure incredibly tasty meat. I would recommend sourcing a vendor that sells heritage breeds of pork (free-range animals with minimum human contact). Try it at least once; you will be delighted by the flavor and texture.

Pork Ribs

While many people consider baby back ribs to be a premium rib, St. Louis–style ribs work better for churrasco cooking, making them the preferred type of pork ribs at Texas de Brazil. St. Louis ribs have more meat between the bones than baby back ribs do, and they usually have part of the belly and brisket on the bones. Baby backs are fine to throw on a flat grill, but if you have to cross them with skewers like we do, it is a challenge because the bones are closer to each other and more difficult to bend. As with pork loin, most of the ribs available at the supermarket or butcher shop are acceptable because they will be cooked slowly over low heat until tender. If you are not using a finishing sauce or glaze, I strongly recommend marinating the ribs overnight.

Pork Sausage

Sausage at a churrascaria is a must. In Brazil, sausage tends to be fattier than in the United States because it will dry out during churrasco cooking. The sausage we use at our restaurants is 50 percent beef and 50 percent pork. In order to duplicate a slightly spicy sausage that I loved while growing up in Brazil, we have ours made to specification by a small company in Texas.

Every nationality has its own sausage, and it is amazing the number of sausage varieties you can find—there are literally thousands of them. Sausages came to be cooked churrasco-style when German and Italian immigrants settled in southern Brazil more than a century ago. The traditional gaucho sausage ingredients are very simple: pork, a lot of pork fat, and salt—no other seasoning. What makes these sausages great is that they use meat from free-range pigs that is chopped by hand with a knife, giving it a coarser texture. Unfortunately, they are almost impossible to find nowadays.

I really love sausages and often make them at home with my kids, but the intense labor and cleanup can be a deterrent to many home cooks. I am a firm believer that you should make sausage from scratch, battling with stuffing and the natural casing, at least once in your life. But if you have to buy sausages, I strongly recommend purchasing them from a reputable butcher

shop that doesn't make a large volume. Shops that make smaller quantities of sausage tend to use any cuts that are left unsold rather than buying cheap scraps of pork meat. Since they only sell top-quality cuts of pork, that is what they will use to make the sausage. Most of the time they use salt and seasoning sparingly, so I suggest placing an order a few days in advance and asking the butcher to be generous with the seasoning and fat.

LAMB CUTS

Lamb Chops

Despite the fact that it is expensive, the lamb chop is one of the most prized meats at a churrascaria. We cut eight-rib racks into eight French-style chops, which means the rib bones are exposed. Because we have to skewer them, we need to buy them large—18/20. This number indicates that each rack will weigh anywhere between 18 and 20 ounces each.

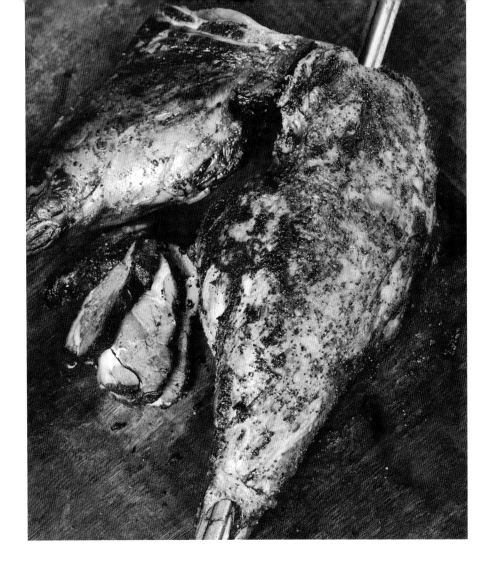

I always prefer fresh lamb, but frozen is equally good. For the best cut, ask your butcher for chops from young lamb, under a year old.

For me, the most desirable characteristic of a lamb chop is its mildness. The meat should be sweet, without any trace of gamey flavor. Not all racks are equal: some breeds of lamb were developed for wool and the meat will be inferior in quality, so be aware of significantly lower prices when shopping. Again, always ask a trustworthy butcher.

Leg of Lamb

While lamb chops are mild, the legs usually have a stronger, more pronounced flavor, almost gamey, and many people prefer them to chops because of this. For the restaurant, we buy semi-boneless leg of lamb because the aitchbone is removed, which makes carving at the table much easier for the servers.

It is interesting to note that we use mostly Australian lamb at Texas de Brazil. American lamb is a phenomenal product, but we cannot use it for a single reason: the domestic animals are much larger than their Australian counterparts, which would make the leg of lamb difficult and exhausting for our carvers to carry around the dining room and serve. Even if the carvers were strong and athletic, the leg of lamb would not fit on the grill since it has to be skewered to cook.

The same tips for buying lamb chops apply to the legs—knowing and trusting a knowledgeable butcher is a must. For those concerned about grass-fed meat, not only is our lamb entirely grass fed, but it is also free range—a very natural product.

CHICKEN CUTS

Chicken breasts and drumsticks are the only two cuts of chicken we serve at our restaurants. (I also love chicken thighs, which are great on skewers over charcoal flames.) Buying chicken is much easier than buying beef, pork, or lamb. Just be sure that the chicken is USDA Grade A and that the skin looks healthy, without bruises or stains. It is worth paying a little more for a chicken labeled "organic" if you are unsure about the provenance of the product. As far as taste though, I honestly don't think that even the best chef in the world would be able to tell the difference. The most important thing is freshness—chicken spoils faster than other meats, so make sure it is fresh.

Chicken is a great blank canvas waiting for seasoning and marinades. Many people ask why we do not serve plain chicken breast, without bacon, and the reason is simple: the bacon not only adds flavor but also prevents the chicken from drying out.

Sauces and Marinades

Not a day goes by that our public relations department doesn't receive an email or call from someone who wants to buy our seasonings and spices. They cannot believe it when we reveal that most of the beef we serve is seasoned simply with salt. The flavor comes from the smoke that is created while the fat renders and drips over the burning charcoal. This is hard to duplicate if you are not cooking over an open flame with wood. However, for chicken, pork, and leg of lamb, we do use a traditional marinade. I don't dismiss the idea that one day you will be able to find our marinade on supermarket shelves, but for now we make it fresh every day in each one of our restaurants—as we do with our chimichurri sauce—and I am glad to share these recipes with you.

Texas de Brazil Marinade

In southern Brazil, every family has a recipe for marinade, but they all usually contain wine, rosemary, sage, and garlic as the basic ingredients. The Texas de Brazil recipe includes a touch of cumin and Dijon mustard, which makes it a versatile, flavor-enhancing marinade for pork, chicken, and lamb (but never for beef cuts since seasoning with salt is the traditional way to prepare beef).

MAKES 2 ½ CUPS
(600 ML)

1 cup (240 ml) red wine (such as Merlot or Cabernet)

12 fresh sage leaves, divided

4 sprigs rosemary, divided

2 stalks scallions

6 cloves garlic

1 tablespoon kosher salt

1 tablespoon Dijon mustard

1 tablespoon dried oregano

1 teaspoon cumin

1 teaspoon dried crushed red pepper

1 cup (240 ml) olive oil or vegetable oil

In a blender, combine the wine, 6 sage leaves, 2 sprigs rosemary, scallions, garlic, salt, mustard, oregano, cumin, and red pepper; blend at low speed until it forms a paste. With the blender still running, slowly add the oil in a thin stream. When the mixture is emulsified, transfer the marinade to an airtight container or jar. Chop the remaining 2 sprigs rosemary and 6 sage leaves and add them to the marinade. The marinade can be kept in the refrigerator for up to 5 days. If the sauce breaks, simply shake the jar before using it.

A tasty way to use this marinade is for roast chicken. Split a roasting chicken in half, season with salt, cover with ½ cup marinade, and let it rest overnight in the refrigerator. Slow roast the chicken over low temperature on a charcoal grill.

Chimichurri Sauce

Chimichurri is not Brazilian at all—we need to give the credit to the Argentinians for creating a fantastic sauce that goes well with many dishes. Traditionally, churrasco is not eaten with sauce. Die-hard gauchos will tell you that all you need to eat with churrasco is a good farinha de mandioca, a very dry flour made from cassava root. But after a trip to Mendoza, Argentina, years ago and trying the authentic sauce with meat, I decided that Texas de Brazil should offer chimichurri. At our Fort Worth location, there are many Argentinians on our staff, so I asked for a good recipe. To my surprise, every single one of them offered up a different chimichurri recipe, which started a debate. That's when I realized there is no such thing as a "traditional" chimichurri sauce. I left the Argentinians to argue among themselves and decided to create the sauce on my own, keeping it as simple and as original as possible. After a few questionable results, I came up with this recipe that, if I may humbly say, is as good as any found in Argentina.

MAKES ABOUT 2 CUPS (475 ML)

½ cup (120 ml) white vinegar

3 tablespoons (45 ml) red wine (optional)

⅓ cup (80 ml) olive oil

1 cup (240 ml) vegetable oil

1 bunch Italian parsley, stems discarded, finely chopped

½ bunch cilantro, stems discarded, finely chopped

2 tablespoons freshly minced garlic

2 tablespoons chopped fresh oregano (optional)

1 teaspoon dried oregano

1 teaspoon dried crushed red pepper

Salt

Combine the vinegar, red wine, and olive oil in a mixing bowl. Add the vegetable oil in a steady stream while whisking with a fork. When blended, add the parsley, cilantro, garlic, fresh and dried oregano, and crushed red pepper. Mix with a spatula or large spoon. (Resist the urge to use a blender or food processor; the consistency and taste are far better when mixed by hand.) Season with salt to taste. Transfer the bowl to the refrigerator for at least 1 hour, but preferably overnight (the chimichurri will taste better when the flavors have more time to blend.) The sauce can be refrigerated in an airtight container for about 7 days. It can be also used as a marinade.

I like to use ziplock bags to marinade smaller pieces of meat. Shake and turn the bag every other hour or so to ensure that all the pieces of meat are covered in sauce and get plenty of flavor.

Essential Tools for a Churrasqueiro

To cook churrasco, the only tool that the early gauchos needed was a good knife. While in the Pampas, that knife was used to slaughter the animal, prepare the meat, make wood skewers from tree branches, and when the meat was cooked and ready to eat, cut pieces of the grilled assado directly from the skewer.

Today, churrasco cooking can be accomplished at home with a few basic grilling tools, some of which you may already have and some of which you can buy or build.

CHURRASQUEIRA

The *churrasqueira* is a Brazilian-style grill, or rotisserie. This is the most important item when cooking churrasco; you cannot use a flat grill if churrasco is your ultimate goal. And don't even think about using gas equipment—not only will the flavor be inferior, but nothing else compares to the experience of seeing a piece of meat getting its golden color from burning charcoal.

Professional churrasqueiras can be found online or imported from Brazil, but they are expensive and heavy. Before you make such a large investment, I suggest building your own using a steel drum (for instructions, see page 81). Over time, you can improve this simple project to accommodate your needs or to match the design of your backyard.

Note that the word *rotisserie* is for a grill that will spin or rotate the skewers. While this is very important in a restaurant, you can grill well without the mechanical parts. In fact, turning the skewers by hand is a big part of the fun.

One of the things I like to brag about most is the size of the churrasqueiras at our restaurants—some of them are 24 feet long. They are custom built in Brazil by a factory back home in Caxias do Sul. This company has been in business for many generations, and though most of its revenue is generated in Brazil, they sell their grills all over the world. The owners have been good friends of mine for many years, and we used to cook churrasco together for our Masonic Lodge meetings.

Displaying the rotisseries is important to Texas de Brazil. Many of our grill stations are visible through glass enclosures so that our guests can see everything, including the gauchos cooking the meats and the charcoal burning in the rotisserie. Our guests get excited when I invite them into the grill station for a quick tour and they get to stand next to the rotisserie. The churrasqueira is big and intimidating, so the characteristic noises of spinning metal gears and chains, and the heat and smell of roasting meat and smoke impregnating every wall, is a thrilling experience for most people, especially men. Some are so captivated that they will joke about requesting a job application.

Our rotisseries are not extremely expensive, high-tech pieces of equipment—quite the opposite. Like classic cars, they lack technology and gadgets that can make your life much easier, but they connect with you in a more intimate way—you have to love her and she has to love you back (and like cars, we gauchos refer to our churrasqueiras as "her" and "she"). They have no thermometers, no sensors, nor even temperature controls. They are simply huge boxes designed to burn charcoal and spin skewers. They must be reliable and built to withstand the extreme heat produced by the natural lump charcoal that we use, which can reach over 1,200°F.

No two rotisseries are alike; like an old brick pizza oven, you need to understand its tempers and moods. The gauchos at the restaurant need to know and be familiar with every inch of her—where to place each skewer, where the hottest spot is for a quick sear, and where to place a large leg of lamb so that it cooks slowly and well. It is not easy or cheap to work with a

charcoal-burning rotisserie. It is also interesting to note that the older the grill, the bolder and more complex the flavor of the cooked meats. Over time, the fire-resistant bricks laid on the bottom and sides of the big box become infused with flavors from the meat drippings, seasonings, and smoke—that flavor is transferred to the meat. Old bricks are highly prized for this reason. When we open a new location, we ship some of the old bricks from an existing grill to mix with new bricks in the new rotisserie. It took some time, but I learned that if we don't mix the bricks when we open a new location, the meats, especially the picanha, won't have the complex flavors and aromas that we desire.

KNIVES

You need a good knife or two. A quality knife is usually expensive, but it's worth the investment because it will last a lifetime, so do not compromise. I love knives; I collect them. I have several good-looking knives made of stainless steel, but recently I am favoring handmade carbon steel knives with bone or antler handles. Carbon steel knives are more difficult to maintain but much easier to sharpen. They have their own personality, and I love the way they feel. If you don't yet have a knife that you love, start with a 9-inch traditional chef's knife. Don't buy it for the look—feel it. With the right weight, it will feel like an extension of your arm.

It amazes me how many people believe that a knife will remain sharp forever without maintenance. You need a good sharpening stone. The best ones have two sides: one side that is medium-coarse and one that is fine, almost like glass. Our guests find it very cool when they see our gauchos sharpening their knives using the sharpening rod. Some of the gauchos are extremely fast, and they make the process look effortless. But it will take you many hours of practice to get that good. If you are up to the challenge, buy one, but know that mastering the process will take time and effort.

A great tool to use is a sharpener with two ceramic discs. They make the job very easy, with good results. Electric knife sharpeners work efficiently, but I would not recommend them. They grind off metal every time you use them, quickly changing your knife in appearance and functionality.

CUTTING BOARDS

I love a good, large cutting board and cannot cook without one. For best results, purchase one that is made out of hardwood, preferably dark wood, and never bamboo. It has to be heavy, no smaller than 12 x 18 inches, and at least 2 inches thick.

The same cutting board that you use to cut the raw beef for the churrasco will be used (after you wash it) to serve the cooked meat. Roasted beef always looks nicer when served on a wooden cutting board. Remember to clean the cutting board very well between uses with hot running water and mild soap. Rinse well and dry it with a paper towel. Another great way to clean your cutting board is to sprinkle a generous amount of salt over it and then rub with half a lemon. It will not only be clean, but it will also smell fresh. Never soak a wooden cutting board in water and never put it in the dishwasher, or you will ruin it forever.

Once a month, apply a good amount of food-grade mineral oil to the cutting board, and let the wood absorb it for about two hours. Use paper towels to blot off any excess oil and the wood will be refreshed again. Cutting boards get better when they begin to show some wear and tear and develop a personality.

SKEWERS

Without skewers, you cannot cook churrasco. If you don't pierce the meat with the skewer, you are cooking something else. It may taste exactly the same, but it is not churrasco.

Skewers are made of stainless steel with a metal or wooden handle. Traditional skewers can be found in two lengths: 19.5 inches (49.5 cm) or 23.5 inches (59.5 cm) from the tip of the skewer to the center of the resting wheel.

The lengths are standard with only two options because the rotisseries are made to accommodate them, but there are many more choices when it comes to the width of the blade. Wider blades will be used for larger pieces like picanha, leg of lamb, and flap meat; medium-sized blades are used for smaller pieces of meat like sausage, chicken breast with bacon, and Parmesan pork; and thin skewers are only used for chicken hearts. There are also some

skewers with two prongs—these are excellent for thick steaks, like rib-eye, but very few churrascarias use them in Brazil.

Skewers are not expensive (unless you buy 1,500 at once, as we do for each restaurant that we open) and you can find many stores online that carry them. Most cooks will be fine ordering twelve skewers—five with the wider blades and seven with the medium blades. If you find a double skewer, buy one of those too. Consider buying two of the thin skewers if you think that you may want to cook chicken hearts someday.

THERMOMETER

You may be surprised, but I think less than 1 percent of homes in Brazil have a food thermometer. When Brazilians roast churrasco, they make a deep incision in the meat with a knife to see if it is cooked through; if it is not, they cook it a little longer and make another incision in a different spot. While this is perfectly fine for those with meat-grilling experience, I do recommend

having a good thermometer—you can easily ruin a large leg of lamb or pork loin if you overcook it.

If you understand the science of carryover cooking, you know the meat keeps cooking even after it's removed from the heat source. The larger or denser the meat, the greater the amount of carryover cooking. However, with the thermometer you can read the exact temperature and remove the skewer from the heat when the thermometer reads about 10 degrees below the desired temperature. This way, as the meat rests, the temperature will keep rising until it is perfectly cooked.

Building Your Own Gaucho Grill

Not everyone in Rio Grande do Sul has a huge, fancy, and shiny stainless-steel piece of equipment in their house or on their apartment's balcony. For grilling churrasco, many gauchos still use an improvised grill made with a steel drum cut lengthwise and adapted to burn the charcoal and hold the skewers. In fact, some of the most memorable churrascos I attended were cooked in this humble and primitive manner. Growing up in Brazil, I used to see them everywhere. Even now, if I close my eyes, I can almost smell the roasted meat and see the light haze from all the grills—that was a clear sign of a happy moment to come, or more precisely, that family and friends would gather at the same table and Sunday lunch would be served.

I have had many joyful moments around one of those modest grills—cooking churrasco, sipping caipirinhas, and chatting with my friends—but I never got around to building one for myself. So, one day I decided to finally build one out of a steel drum. Once it was finished, I carted it over to our corporate office parking lot and grilled some garlic picanha, sausage, and chicken breasts with bacon. It was a nice spring day, so I set up some tables with bread, potato salad, and disposable plates for an impromptu company lunch. Everyone loved it and came away with a sense of what I used to experience as a kid. I enjoyed cooking for the staff so much that I decided to leave the grill at the office and build another one for my own backyard.

It's actually simple to build this grill. You don't need technical know-how and I promise it really works. Of course it's helpful to have a few basic tools to cut metal and some welding skills, but if you don't, or don't feel up to the task, simply obtain these parts and go to a local metal shop with these instructions and pictures. They will be able to make one for you in just a few hours.

MATERIALS

1 (55-gallon) open-head steel drum (about 34 inches high x 22 inches in diameter)

About 72 feet square steel tubing (1½ inches high x 1½ inches wide x ⅟₁₆ inch thick)

INSTRUCTIONS

For the Drum:

1. Start by standing the 55-gallon drum up and cutting it in half from top to bottom so that it is divided into 2 equal halves resembling clamshells (see photo). *Caution:* Before cutting the drum, be sure that no flammables or fumes are inside. Under certain conditions, sparks from cutting the barrel could ignite a fire.

2. Weld the two drum pieces together horizontally so that the open sides are connected. The split and welded barrel should then be approximately 68 inches long x 22 inches wide x 11 inches deep.

For the Frame:

Using the steel tubing, you will need to create the frame and support for the barrel. The measurements below are approximate. Create your own "shop drawings" and double check the measurements before you start cutting the metal tubes.

1. Measure and cut 4 pieces of the steel tubing, each 48 inches. These will become the vertical legs of the frame.

2. Measure and cut 7 pieces of the steel tubing, each 68 inches. One of them will be used under the barrel to support it. The other 6 will be used for 3 support shelves.

3. Measure and cut 6 pieces of the steel tubing, each 22 inches. These will be the horizontal side supports.

To Assemble:

1. Start by building 2 H-shaped structures that will become the sides of the grill. The H-support is made by 2 vertical 48-inch tubes and one 22½-inch horizontal tube welded 16½ inches from the ground.

2. Connect the two H supports with a 64½-inch metal tube and place the split barrel on top.

3. Weld the vertical parts as shown in the photograph.

4. Finally, you can paint it or leave it the way it is, but I strongly suggest painting it because it will look much nicer. If painting, only use heat-resistant paint, which can be found in your local home improvement store. *Do not paint the interior of the barrel where the charcoal will burn.* When buying the paint for this grill, it is best to choose black and gray—the gaucho in me will be disappointed if you paint the grill in vibrant tropical colors.

The Four-Armed Cross Spit

If you're feeling ambitious enough to cook in a fire pit and want to prepare a whole animal or larger sections of an animal, like a whole beef rib, suckling pig, or whole lamb (see recipe on page 116), you can build a four-armed cross spit. This large metal spit is placed vertically into the ground next to a pit fire. The cooking time is very long, usually 4 hours or more depending on the size of the meat, so you should reserve this adventure for when you have a large group and can make it a long afternoon or evening event.

There are hundreds of variations for a spit like this, but this version is very simple and inexpensive to make using materials easily found at your home improvement store.

MATERIALS

2 (48-inch) steel rebars (½ inch diameter)

1 (5-foot) steel T-post (approximately 1 x 1½ inches)

INSTRUCTIONS

1. Cut the first rebar into one 18-inch piece and one 30-inch piece. Repeat with the other rebar.

2. Using a metal saw, cut the end of the T-post at a 25-degree angle to form an acute tip.

3. Secure the T-post with the flat side facing up. Measure and mark 5 inches inward from the uncut side of the post. Measure the center of one 30-inch rebar and weld it perpendicularly against the post.

4. Measure a further 8 inches down the post and weld the first 18-inch rebar, centered.

5. Measure another 8 inches down the post and weld the remaining 30-inch rebar, centered.

6. Measure a final 8 inches down the post and weld the last 18-inch rebar.

7. Use a metal grinder to smooth out the welded spots and any rough areas.

10 Important Churrasco Grilling Tips

I am regularly asked for tips on how to grill meat churrasco style, so here are my top ten:

1. When buying beef, look for cuts with good marbleization and a cap of fat. Lean cuts don't work.

2. In any churrascaria, the most requested cut of beef is picanha, also called coulotte. Ask your butcher for the cap of the top sirloin, fat on.

3. For lamb, chicken, and pork, create your own marinade by combining olive oil, wine or beer with garlic, green herbs, and a hot element like black pepper or crushed red pepper.

4. To enhance the flavor of lamb, chicken, and pork, marinate overnight.

5. Use good-quality lump charcoal (it's the key to getting that smoky grilled flavor). Never use chemical fire starters, or else your meat will taste like kerosene.

6. Wait until the charcoal is completely burned—minus black fumes—before grilling. The charcoal must be glowing and covered with white ash.

7. Cover the beef cuts with salt just seconds before placing over the open flame—never rub the salt into the meat.

8. Grill the meat about 12 inches above the charcoal—the flames should not touch the meat.

9. To get the best-tasting churrasco, cook the meat until its external cap of fat is golden brown. Pale or grayish-colored fat will result in a bland churrasco.

10. Large pieces of meat, especially beef and lamb, need to rest after cooking so that the juices have a chance to stabilize. After the meat is cooked, move the skewer to a cooler area of the grill so that it will stay warm until ready to eat without cooking further.

Like any skill, culinary or not, you will improve over time and with practice. Keep experimenting. Cook the same food many times until you feel comfortable doing it and can control all the variables. Your first few attempts at churrasco may not be very impressive, but if you have the passion to master this technique, you will learn from the mistakes and eventually succeed at grilling and serving up this sumptuous and savory fare. Then watch out—as the rich aromas waft from your backyard, your neighbors will be clamoring to attend a barbecue at your house.

TRADITIONAL GAUCHO CUISINE

Gaucho Kebabs
Xixo Gaucho, 90

Beef on a Plow Blade
Bife na Chapa, 93

Bauru-Style Steak
Bauru ao Prato, 94

Beef Tenderloin with Hearts of Palm and Cheese
Filet com Palmito e Queijo, 97

Braised Rolled Beef
Matambre Recheado, 98

Fire-Roasted Picanha
Picanha Assada no Fogo, 100

Oven-Roasted Picanha
Picanha Assada no Forno, 103

Picanha with Horseradish and Garlic
Picanha com Raiz Forte e Alho, 104

Fried Beef Empanada
Pastel Frito de Carne, 106

Beef-Bone Stock
Caldo de Res, 109

Caramelized Squash
Moranga Caramelada, 110

Boiled Beef with Horseradish-Vinegar Sauce
Carne Alessa com Cren, 113

Pork Ribs with Yucca Flour
Costela de Porco com Farinha, 114

Lamb Roasted on the Ground
Ovelha Assada no Chão, 116

Chicken Stew with Soft Polenta
Galinha com Polenta Mole, 118

Brazilian Chicken Salad
Salpicão de Frango, 121

Chicken Thighs with Beer
Sobrecoxa de Frango com Cerveja, 122

Chicken Hearts
Coração de Frango, 125

Chicken "Drumstick" Fritter
Coxinha de Frango, 126

Bucatini with Quail Sauce
Bucatini com Molho de Codorna, 129

Whole Fish Baked on a Roof Tile
Tainha na Telha, 130

Oven-Roasted Salted Cod
Bacalhau ao Forno, 132

Codfish Fritters
Bolinho de Bacalhau, 135

Cold Savory Torte
Torta Fria, 136

Squash Ravioli
Tortei de Moranga, 138

Spinach Cannelloni
Canelone de Espinafre, 140

Collard Greens with Bacon
Couve com Toicinho, 142

Dandelion Greens with Bacon
Radicci com Toicinho, 145

Fried Polenta Stuffed with Cheese
Polenta Frita Recheada com Queijo, 146

Seasoned Cassava Flour
Farofa Gaucha, 149

Wagoners' Rice
Arroz Carreteiro, 150

Cattlemen's Beans
Feijão Tropeiro, 153

Brazilian Vinaigrette
Vinagrete/Molho Campeiro, 154

Chocolate Truffles
Brigadeiro, 157

Dulce de Leche/ Caramelized Milk
Doce de Leite, 158

Gaucho Kebabs
Xixo Gaucho

When pronounced in Portuguese, the word xixo is "shi-sho," probably originating from a way to say "shish" in "shish kebab." Kebabs are pretty popular in southern Brazil, even though it's rare for a gaucho to cook vegetables on a skewer right next to meat. There are no Middle Eastern seasonings used in this recipe since they are hard to come by and unfamiliar to locals in southern Brazil, but the combination of grilling different meats and vegetables together on a skewer creates plenty of flavor. Xixos are great to cook when you are serving many people with different food preferences. They are also convenient—you cook a few different skewers, serve them on a large platter, and guests can grab what they like the most, whether it's chicken, vegetables, beef, or pork. While there are no traditional ways to prepare and cook kebabs in Brazil, don't expect beef to be medium-rare—all cuts will be well done. In this recipe, the vegetables and bacon will help prevent the meat from drying out.

SERVES 12

1 kabocha squash or other winter squash (such as butternut)

2 medium yellow onions

1 lb (450 g) chicken breast

1 lb (450 g) beef sirloin or similar cut (such as tenderloin or tri-tip)

1 lb (450 g) pork loin

1 lb (450 g) kielbasa sausage

½ lb (230 g) bacon, cut into 2 in (5 cm) slices

4 medium tomatoes, quartered and seeded

2 medium green bell peppers, cut into 2 in (5 cm) pieces

1 cup Texas de Brazil Marinade (page 71)

Salt

Rice, for serving

Quarter the squash and reserve 3 of the quarters for another purpose. Peel the squash, cut into ½-inch-thick (13-mm) slices, and cut the slices into 2-inch (5-cm) pieces. Peel and cut the onions in half and then in half again, opening each section by hand to fan the layers. Cut the chicken breast, beef sirloin, and pork loin into 2-inch (5-cm) squares, each about ¾ inch (19 mm) thick. Cut the sausage into 2-inch-long (5-cm) pieces.

Place all of the ingredients together in a large mixing bowl and sprinkle with some salt. Add the marinade, toss gently, cover, and let it rest together in the refrigerator overnight.

Prepare the grill by heating up lump charcoal until fully burned, but with no black fumes.

While the charcoal is heating, take 6 long skewers and prepare the kebabs by skewering pieces of meat, vegetables, and bacon in a random fashion. Create different combinations, but make sure the bacon is always placed between 2 pieces of meat. Place the skewers on the grill about 15 inches (38 cm) from the charcoal (at medium heat), and turn them frequently until the squash is tender and the meat is fully cooked and showing some char, about 35 minutes. Using a pair of tongs, slide the meat from the skewer to a large platter. Serve over rice if desired.

Beef on a Plow Blade
Bife na Chapa

Round plow blades are found everywhere in Rio Grande do Sul. Like in Argentina and Uruguay, huge crops of grains such as wheat and soy are commonplace. For many years, gauchos have taken these large plow blades and turned them into skillets called disco de arado to quickly sear thin slices of beef, usually rib-eyes. To build these rustic frying pans, they weld together the holes on the plow blade, attach two handles for easy maneuvering, and then grind the whole surface. The plow blades desired for this purpose are very old ones with many years of use. The gauchos contend that the blade's years of contact with the earth and the metal's characteristics add a special flavor to the meat. If you're handy and adventurous, you can create your own disco de arado; otherwise, you can buy one online or use a large cast-iron skillet. I love to make sandwiches with this steak. Use the hot skillet to toast split baguettes. The toasted bread will absorb all the juices from the meat, onions, and sauce.

SERVES 8

For the grill:

3 large rocks (similar in size)

10 lb (4.5 kg) firewood

Disco de arado or a large, heavy skillet

Long metal tongs

For the beef:

2 ripe tomatoes, finely chopped, or ½ cup (120 ml) good-quality tomato sauce (if ripe tomatoes are not available)

Salt

1 teaspoon dried oregano or a few sprigs fresh oregano

½ cup (120 ml) red wine (optional)

8 rib-eye steaks

Freshly ground white pepper

1 cup (120 ml) red wine vinegar or white wine vinegar

¾ cup (180 ml) vegetable oil

4 yellow onions, cut into ½-in (13-mm) strips

To build the fire pit, place the rocks on the ground approximately 12 inches (30 cm) apart (and well away from any combustible structure), forming a level triangular base; this is where the disco de arado or skillet will rest. In the center space between the rocks, arrange and light a few logs of the firewood. (Alternatively, you can use a strong single-burner stove, available at camping stores.)

To prepare the beef, put the tomatoes in a small bowl, season with salt and oregano, add the red wine, and set aside. Remove any excess fat from the rib-eye steaks, and then season them with salt and white pepper. Transfer the seasoned steaks to a mixing bowl and add the vinegar. Turn the meat over several times to absorb the liquid; allow the steaks to marinate for at least 15 minutes but not more than 30 minutes.

Spread the burning wood flat and level between the three rocks. Place the disco de arado or skillet over the wood, balancing on the rocks. Add more wood under the skillet if needed. While the skillet is heating, pour the oil over the beef in the mixing bowl and toss to cover. Allow the skillet to become extremely hot, then carefully place the steaks flat and open on the skillet, avoiding any overlap, and drizzle any remaining oil over the steaks. Using a long pair of tongs, turn the steaks over once they form a nice crust, about 3 minutes. Move the steaks to the side of the skillet so that the oil and meat juices flow to the middle, and then add the onions to the center and sauté until golden. Transfer the steaks and onions to a serving platter. Add the tomatoes to the skillet and cook for 1 to 2 minutes to form a thin sauce. With a long spoon, pour the sauce over the steak and onions.

Bauru-Style Steak
Bauru ao Prato

This is one of my favorite dishes of all time. I love everything in it: beef, cheese, ham, tomato, and olive oil. Best of all, it can easily be shared with family or friends. Some restaurants in my hometown specialize in this dish and serve it family style, accompanied by white rice, French fries, and a green salad. Mastering the preparation may take practice, but I assure you that once you get it right, you will be delighted. My wife and I usually serve this when we want to impress dinner guests, and they always ask for the recipe.

SERVES 8

4–6 medium ripe tomatoes, thickly sliced

Salt

Dried oregano

½ cup (120 ml) olive oil, divided

8 (6 oz/170 g] beef tenderloin steaks (about ¾ in/19 mm thick)

Freshly ground black pepper

1 large yellow onion, thickly sliced

5 stalks scallions, chopped

8 thick slices mozzarella

8 slices salty ham (do not use honey ham or other sweet hams)

Rice, for serving

French fries, for serving

Preheat oven to 400°F.

Place the tomato slices on a sheet pan and season with salt and oregano. Drizzle with some of the olive oil and bake for 5 to 10 minutes, or until char marks appear. Remove the tomatoes from the oven and let them rest. Reduce the oven temperature to 350°F.

Season the steak generously with salt and pepper. Heat 3 to 4 tablespoons of the remaining olive oil in a 12- or 14-inch (30- or 36-cm) cast-iron skillet. When the skillet is very hot and the oil is smoking, sear the steaks in 2 batches. Cook the steaks for 3 minutes on each side (don't worry about them being underdone—you will finish cooking them in the oven). Transfer the steaks to a plate and reserve. Using the same hot skillet, sauté the onion and the scallions until golden but still firm. Season with salt and oregano, turn off the heat, and transfer the onions to a plate and reserve.

Place the steaks with their juices back in the skillet, side by side. Cover each steak with 1 mozzarella slice, and then cover the mozzarella with 1 ham slice (it is okay if the cheese and ham overlap on the steaks in the skillet). Cover the steaks with the charred tomatoes and the sautéed onions, including all their juices, and then drizzle with the remaining olive oil. Bake the steaks uncovered for about 15 minutes, or until the juices on the bottom of the skillet start to bubble and the steaks are cooked to your liking. When serving, pour some of the delicious juices over each steak. Serve with sides of rice and French fries.

The leftover steak heats well in the microwave, so whether hot or cold, you can create one of the best sandwiches you'll ever eat!

Beef Tenderloin with Hearts of Palm and Cheese
Filet com Palmito e Queijo

I remember the first time I went to Lancheria Andrea, a small, casual, and unpretentious family-run restaurant in my hometown. I was about sixteen years old and working for a manufacturing company. One night, we had to work late to finish shipping a large order, and at the end of the shift, our boss took us for a late dinner. It was at Lancheria Andrea that I had one of the best steaks I ever ate, loaded with mozzarella cheese, hearts of palm, white asparagus, bacon, butter, and peas. Accompanying the steak were unlimited portions of polenta with quail sauce, spaghetti with chicken gizzards, fried polenta, fried eggs, a radicchio salad with bacon, and French fries—just amazing.

The steak is oven-baked in a skillet, retaining the juices from the butter, steak, and bacon. I always thought that this dish was too unusual to be appreciated by Americans, but whenever I've served it to friends, they were crazy about it and went on to re-create the dish in their own kitchens. Try this for yourself—you'll be glad you did.

SERVES 4 TO 6

1 (2 lb/900 g) center-cut beef tenderloin

Salt and freshly ground black pepper

3 tablespoons (45 ml) vegetable oil

12 ounces (340 g) good-quality mozzarella, thickly sliced

8 slices lightly smoked bacon

1 stick (113 g) butter, cut into pats

8 spears white asparagus, blanched until soft, or canned white asparagus

8 hearts of palm, cut into ¼-in (6-mm) slices

1 cup (150 g) frozen green peas, defrosted and uncooked

Preheat the oven to 400°F.

Trim away all fat and silver skin from the tenderloin. Place the meat on a cutting board, and using a meat tenderizer or the bottom of a heavy frying pan, pound the steak a few times to flatten it out to about 1½ to 2 inches (4 to 5 cm) in thickness. Season the beef generously with salt and pepper.

Heat the oil in a heavy skillet just slightly larger than the flattened steak. When the skillet is very hot, sear the steak for about 5 minutes on each side, forming a nice crust on the outside but keeping the center rare. Remove the skillet from the stove, cover the tenderloin with the mozzarella, and top it with the bacon and butter. Arrange the asparagus, hearts of palm, and peas around the steak in the skillet. Bake in the middle of the oven for about 15 minutes for a medium to medium-rare center, making sure the bacon is fully cooked and the cheese is melted. Remove from the oven and let it rest for about 10 minutes before serving.

Braised Rolled Beef
Matambre Recheado

Gauchos from Argentina, Uruguay, and southern Brazil love this dish, but it is almost unknown in other parts of Brazil. In Spanish, mata hambre means "hunger killer." This is one of my favorite meals, and every time I visit my family, my mother knows that I will be expecting it. This dish takes time to prepare, but it is truly worth the effort. Part of the challenge is finding rose meat, which is an extremely tough cap of meat between the cow's ribs and skin. Only a few butchers will be familiar with it, but if you have a Mexican butcher or carniceria nearby, ask for the "suadero"—there is a good chance they will have it. If not, substitute with flap steak and pound evenly. Make sure you have a roll of cooking twine on hand for tying the meat.

SERVES 4 TO 6

1 large piece of rose meat (weighing about 3 lb/1.5 kg and measuring about 15 x 8 in/38 x 20 cm when spread open), trimmed of all fat

Salt and freshly ground black pepper

½ lb (230 g) ground beef

2 small yellow onions, chopped, divided

1 long kielbasa or andouille sausage

4 small carrots, peeled and cut lengthwise into sticks

4 hard-boiled eggs, peeled and halved

2 slices bacon

6 stalks scallions

3 tablespoons (45 ml) vegetable oil

1 cup (240 ml) tomato puree

2 cups (475 ml) water

Open the rose meat on a flat surface. Trim the edges to create a rectangle. Season the meat with salt and pepper. In a bowl, mix the ground beef with half of the chopped onion, and season the mixture with salt and pepper. Spread the beef mixture lengthwise over the rose meat in a 3-inch-wide (7.5 cm) line. Lengthwise on top of the ground beef, place the sausage, carrots, eggs, bacon, and scallions. Roll up the meat tightly as if preparing a sushi roll or Swiss roll. Tie the roll of meat with about 4 feet of cooking twine, and season it with a generous amount of salt and pepper.

In a large cast-iron Dutch oven, heat the oil over a high flame until hot. Sear the matambre until golden, turning on all sides to brown evenly, about 5 minutes on each side. This very important step will form a nice crust on the meat. Using kitchen tongs, remove the matambre from the pot and let it rest on a cutting board.

Sauté the remaining onions in the same pot until golden, then add the tomato puree. Stir and cook the tomato and onion for about 3 minutes. When heated through, stir in the water and place the matambre back into the Dutch oven—the liquid should be 1 to 2 inches (2.5 to 5 cm) below the top of the meat. Cover and slowly simmer the meat for about 3 hours, checking the liquid content every 30 minutes. If the water evaporates too quickly, add more water. Each time you check the liquid, turn over the matambre so that it cooks evenly. Once the meat is cooked through and tender, remove the lid and let the liquid reduce to the consistency of a marinara sauce. Remove the meat from the pot and place it on a cutting board. Remove the twine and cut the roll into 1-inch-thick (2.5-cm) slices. Spoon the tomato sauce over the meat and serve.

The sliced matambre is good enough to eat without any of its sauce. Reserve the sauce for a side dish of pasta, generally rigatoni, coated with the rich sauce and plenty of Parmesan. It will be one of the best pasta-and-meat combinations you will ever try. You can also thinly slice leftover matambre for a sandwich—it's delicious whether served cold or hot.

Fire-Roasted Picanha
Picanha Assada no Fogo

In Brazil, picanha (known as the sirloin cap or coulotte in the United States) is the preferred cut of beef for churrasco and needs no seasoning other than salt to bring out its natural flavor. This is not the type of meal that can be prepared or eaten quickly, so why not make it a big event? Invite over some friends or family and cook other skewers of meat—sausages, chicken drumsticks, pork, and lamb—at the same time to add variety to this sumptuous meal.

SERVES 4 TO 6

1 whole picanha (about 3 lb/1.5 kg)

4 tablespoons kosher salt

Prepare the grill using about 10 pounds (4.5 kg) of lump charcoal. Before cooking the meat, the charcoal needs to be glowing with little flames and minimal black smoke—this takes approximately 30 minutes to achieve. If white ashes form over the charcoal, gently rotate them with a shovel or other long-handled tool.

To prepare the meat, pat both sides of the picanha dry with a paper towel. Place the picanha fat side up on a cutting board. Using a sharp knife, trim the fat cap to about ¼ to ½ inch (6 to 13 mm) thick (see page 58). Turn over the picanha and remove any silver skin and connective tissues from the bottom. Turn the picanha over again, fat side up, and cut it in half. On the first half of the picanha, cut off the ends of each strip in order to make 2 straight rectangles (one of the pieces will be longer, which is fine). Repeat the process with the other half of the picanha. In total, you should have 4 rectangles and about 10 small pieces cut from the corners—you can use these corners to make Garlic Picanha (page 165).

Take the largest piece of picanha, fold it in the shape of a C (see photos), and skewer it using a stainless-steel skewer. Repeat the process from the largest to the smallest piece. (The reason for starting with the largest piece is that the smallest one will cook a little more and hold the other pieces in place once the skewer is brought to a vertical position.) Over a sink or the cutting board, apply enough kosher salt to slightly cover all sides of the meat, including the fat.

Bring the skewer to rest on the grill, and cook the picanha over the hot and glowing charcoals. The meat should be about 10 inches (25 cm) from the charcoal, and the flames should not touch the meat. If the grill doesn't give you the option to place the meat lower or higher, you can move the charcoals under or away from the meat to control the amount of heat. Turn the skewer about once per minute. You will know you have the perfect temperature when, after a few minutes, the cap of fat is bubbling and starting to melt away. The cap will turn a beautiful golden-brown color, and the melted fat will moisten the meat.

When cooking picanha, gauchos usually don't worry about the internal temperature of the meat. Once the fat cap is golden brown, they will carve the sides of the meat and serve, apply a little more salt, and return the remainder to the fire. They repeat this process until all the meat is consumed, but you can cook the picanha until it reaches the desired internal temperature, remove from the fire, let it rest, and slice it on a wooden cutting board.

Oven-Roasted Picanha

Picanha Assada no Forno

The ideal way of cooking picanha is over an open-flame grill with natural wood charcoal, not only because of the taste but also because of the whole experience. It is always a special event when you and your friends are outside carefully tending a fire and roasting meats while drinking a glass of wine or beer, engaging in great conversations, and telling jokes. The warmth of the fire and the aroma coming from the fat dripping over the glowing embers creates an environment in which to relax and unwind—at least for me. However, oven-roasted picanha is an excellent alternative for those who prefer to cook indoors with much less labor involved. This is an easy way to satisfy your cravings for picanha until you're ready and ambitious enough to build your own grill.

SERVES 4 TO 6

1 whole picanha (about 2½ lb/1 kg)

Freshly ground black pepper

6 tablespoons kosher salt

Preheat the oven to 250°F.

Pat the picanha dry with a paper towel. Place the picanha fat side up on a cutting board. Using a sharp knife, carefully trim the fat cap to about ¼ inch (6 mm) thick. (While this may seem like too much fat, it will melt away as the meat cooks.) Turn the picanha over and remove any silver skin from the bottom of the meat. Season generously with pepper and salt on all sides of the beef—you should be able to see the salt crystals on the meat.

Place the picanha fat side up in a roasting pan or cast-iron skillet that is slightly larger than the meat. Bake in the middle of the oven for about 25 minutes, until the internal temperature is about 110°F; by then, the meat will look grayish and the fat will not show any color. Remove the picanha from the oven and cover loosely with aluminum foil to keep warm.

Turn up the oven to the broil setting and wait until the temperature reaches at least 500°F—the oven needs to be very hot. If necessary, adjust the rack so that the meat will sit 8 to 10 inches (20 to 25 cm) away from the top of the oven. When the oven reaches optimum temperature, quickly remove the aluminum foil and place the meat back in the oven. Broil for 7 to 12 minutes, checking the meat closely and often. The fat should turn a dark golden color, but it can burn very quickly if you don't pay attention. Let the meat get as much color as possible; only remove it from the oven when it turns mahogany brown in color. After removing from the oven, let the meat rest for 10 minutes or longer. An extended period of resting makes some cuts of beef more tender, and it stabilizes the natural juices so that less will run when you carve the meat. After it rests, transfer the meat to a wooden cutting board and serve.

Picanha with Horseradish and Garlic
Picanha com Raiz Forte e Alho

This is an old family recipe. I prepare it whenever I feel a bit homesick, and I want to share it here for nostalgic reasons. This preparation is not common in Brazil because horseradish is only consumed as a condiment mixed with red vinegar and usually served with boiled beef. This version is served with roasted beef. The spiciness of the horseradish balances the richness of fatty meats, and the garlic and herbs add extra layers of flavor. It is an easy dish to prepare, and it makes for an elegant presentation, especially if accompanied by roasted potatoes.

SERVES 4

15 large cloves garlic

½ cup plus 2 tablespoons (150 ml) vegetable oil, divided

Freshly ground black pepper

Kosher salt

½ cup strained and squeezed bottled white horseradish

½ cup (12 g) chopped fresh parsley or chives

1 large picanha (about 3 lb/1.5 kg)

Preheat the oven to 300°F.

In a small pot, add the garlic cloves and cover with ½ cup of oil. Cook on the stove over low heat until the garlic completely softens. Remove from heat and let cool. Once the garlic is cool, remove the cloves from the oil with a slotted spoon and place in a bowl. (You can reserve the remaining garlic-infused oil for bread or for use in other recipes). Smash the garlic with a fork, then season with pepper and 1 tablespoon of kosher salt. Add the horseradish, parsley, and the remaining 2 tablespoons oil. Stir and set aside.

Place the picanha on a cutting board, and use a sharp knife to trim the fat cap to about ¼ inch (6 mm) thick. Remove any silver skin from the bottom side of the meat. Use a large knife to cut a C-shaped pocket going almost all the way from the thickest side of the picanha to the opposite tip. Using your fingers, insert the horseradish and garlic mixture evenly inside the pocket. Sprinkle some pepper over the fat cap, and season all sides of the meat generously with salt. Place the meat in a roasting pan with the fat facing up. Bake the picanha for about 25 minutes. Remove the pan from the oven and increase the heat to 450°F. Cover the meat with aluminum foil while waiting for the oven temperature to increase. Once the temperature reaches 450°F, remove the foil and return the pan to the oven for about 5 minutes—just enough time for the fat cap to turn deep brown. Remove from the oven and let the meat rest for at least 15 minutes before slicing.

Fried Beef Empanada
Pastel Frito de Carne

In Brazil, a pastel is a small deep-fried pie, just like an empanada, that is usually filled with ground beef or cheese and ham. Pastéis (plural of pastel) are extremely popular in Brazil, Argentina, and many other countries in South and Central America. However, in Brazil they are always deep-fried, while in Argentina and many other countries, they are oven-baked. Pastéis are never a meal; instead, they are a delicious snack that is usually eaten while drinking beer or wine. The tricky part of making a pastel is the dough; when done right, it will be crispy, it will have the right amount of bubbles, and it will be perfectly golden in color when cooked. However, if time and patience are short, you can buy frozen empanada dough.

Pastéis can be filled with almost anything. Hearts of palm and cheese are favorites among Brazilians. I love chopped ham and cheese together. Canned tuna, onions, and seeded tomatoes work well too. During a trip to Buenos Aires, I had one of the best empanadas ever—a perfect crust filled with Gorgonzola and walnuts. Many roadside churrascarias in my home state make pastéis using the leftover meat from the churrasco and serve them the next morning to truck drivers or travelers. I have fond memories of stopping at one of these humble churrascarias on the way to the beach during summer vacations to have a pastel and coffee with milk served in a glass.

MAKES ABOUT 20 EMPANADAS

For the dough:

3 cups (360 g) all-purpose flour

1½ tablespoons salt

1 tablespoon (15 ml) cachaça or vodka (optional)

3 tablespoons (45 ml) vegetable oil

2 cups (475 ml) cold water

For the filling:

2 tablespoons (30 ml) vegetable oil

1 lb (450 g) ground beef (85 percent lean/15 percent fat)

½ small yellow onion, finely chopped

2 cloves garlic, minced

2 large eggs, beaten

1 tablespoon kosher salt

1 teaspoon white pepper

¼ cup (45 g) coarsely chopped good-quality olives,

3 tablespoons chopped fresh Italian parsley

Vegetable oil, for frying

To make the dough, mix together the flour and salt in a large bowl. Pour in the cachaça and oil, then slowly add the water, mixing the dough in circles with your hands. When well mixed, transfer the dough to a lightly floured surface and knead for about 3 minutes. When necessary, add more water or flour and work the dough until smooth and elastic, like the consistency of fresh pasta. Transfer the dough to a bowl, cover with plastic, and let it rest in the refrigerator for about 30 minutes.

To make the filling, heat the oil in a skillet over medium heat. Add the meat, onion, and garlic and cook until all juices from the meat and onion evaporate and the meat starts to brown. Push the meat to the sides of the skillet to clear the bottom, then pour the eggs into the center of the skillet and cook until firm. Add the salt, pepper, olives, and parsley to the skillet, mixing all the ingredients together and making sure to break up and incorporate the cooked eggs.

Heat 3 inches of oil to 350°F in a pot or electric fryer.

To make the pastéis, remove the dough from the refrigerator. Using a pasta machine, work the dough to make large sheets of pasta about 15 inches long x 5 inches wide x $\frac{1}{16}$ inch thick (38 cm x 13 cm x 1.6 mm). Lay the pasta sheets on a lightly floured surface. Using a small bowl or cup and a paring knife, cut discs between 4 and 6 inches (10 and 15 cm) in diameter. Knead the excess trimmings together to make more sheets of dough, then cut into disks. You can also use a pasta pin.

In the middle of each disk, add 1 to 2 tablespoons of the filling. Fold over to form a half-moon shape, and then seal the edges together with a fork. If the dough gets dry, you can moisten the edges slightly with a wet pastry brush. Repeat until all of the filling is used.

Fry a few pastéis at a time for 3 to 4 minutes, until golden brown. Remove from the oil and drain on paper towels before serving.

If you find the process of making your own dough daunting, use store-bought empanada dough, which is available in the freezer section at most Latin groceries and large supermarkets. The dough comes in disks that are ready to be filled and fried.

Beef-Bone Stock
Caldo de Res

In southern Brazil, it is a common practice to use the leftover bones from the churrasco to make a tasty broth. When I was growing up, Monday's lunch would most likely be a soup made from the charred bones of Sunday's lunch. We go through hundreds of beef ribs at Texas de Brazil each week. I often ask our chef in Dallas to save the bones from the ribs we prepare in the kitchen so that I can make stock at home. If you don't have leftover bones, ask your butcher for the side chain of the rib-eye—it has a nice combination of bone, meat, and cartilage. This broth is nutritious and rich in proteins. In fact, many people believe that bone broth speeds up the healing process during illness—plus, it's wonderfully soothing. I cook pasta with the broth, use it for risottos, or—even better—simply heat and drink it in a large coffee mug on a cold winter night. It is steak in a liquid form. It takes several hours to make, but this broth is so versatile and delicious that it's worth the time and effort.

MAKES 4 TO 5 QUARTS
(3.75 TO 4.75 L)

6–7 lb (2.7–3 kg) beef bones, preferably cut into small pieces to reveal the interior

2 unpeeled onions, quartered

½ lb (230 g) white mushrooms or shiitake mushrooms, roughly chopped

2 large carrots, roughly chopped

6 cloves garlic

½ cup (120 ml) soy sauce

⅓ cup (60 g) kosher salt, plus more as needed

1 bunch scallions, chopped

1 bunch parsley, chopped

1 stalk celery, chopped

1 oz (28 g) black peppercorns

2 gal (7.5 l) water, room temperature

Preheat the oven to 375°F.

Place the bones in a single layer in a roasting pan, and roast them in the oven until nicely browned, about 30 minutes. Transfer the bones and any liquid rendered (including fat) to a stockpot large enough to accommodate all the ingredients (a 15- to 16-quart stockpot will do). Add all of the remaining ingredients, making sure the bones are covered with water. Bring to a boil and reduce to a gentle simmer for 4 to 6 hours, partially covered. A slight reduction is normal and expected, but if you see that the liquid is evaporating too much, add a little water and reduce the heat.

Remove the pot from the heat. Use a long pair of tongs to remove and discard the bones and larger pieces of vegetables. Strain the liquid and taste it, adding more salt if needed. Allow the stock to cool, and then refrigerate it for several hours or overnight. Once the stock is chilled, the fat will float to the top and solidify. Using a flat, slotted spatula, remove the fat and discard or reserve it for cooking. Pour the stock into airtight containers and refrigerate. It can also be stored in the freezer for up to 4 months. (One- or 2-cup containers are easy to store and let you thaw just the amount you need.)

Don't worry if your stock becomes gelatinous after cooling; this is actually a sign of a great homemade stock. Once you heat it, it will turn to liquid.

Caramelized Squash
Moranga Caramelada

If you like sweet potato casserole, you will love this extremely easy-to-make recipe. Brazil has an abundance of sugar cane, which is the basis of cachaça, so cooking squash in sugar syrup is quite popular. While it is on the sweet side, this dish is not necessarily considered a dessert. In the southern parts of Brazil, it is always eaten along with meat, feijoada, and collard greens. It is also delicious served warm with a dollop of sour cream.

SERVES 4 TO 6

1 medium kabocha squash

3 cups (600 g) sugar

1 stick cinnamon

Pinch of salt

3 whole cloves

Pinch of nutmeg

2 cups (475 ml) water

Wash the squash and dry with a kitchen towel. Cut about ½ inch (13 mm) off the top of the squash to make it flat. Lay the squash flat end down on a cutting board and cut into 8 to 12 symmetrical wedges. Using a spoon, remove and discard the seeds from each wedge.

In a 10- to 12-inch (25- to 35-cm) pan over medium heat, melt the sugar and let it cook, stirring occasionally, until it becomes an amber-colored caramel. Add the cinnamon, salt, cloves, and nutmeg, then carefully add the water and stir to dissolve any sugar lumps. Arrange the squash wedges in a single layer in the pan. The syrup should cover the squash about halfway. Cook over medium heat, uncovered, until the underside of the squash is tender, about 15 minutes. With a spatula or kitchen tongs, gently turn the squash pieces over and cook for another 10 minutes, or until both sides are tender and glazed in caramel. Transfer the squash to a serving platter using a slotted spatula and serve it hot or warm. The remaining caramel syrup can be stored in the refrigerator for up to 7 days.

Boiled Beef with Horseradish-Vinegar Sauce

Carne Alessa com Cren

During my first week in the United States, I was served a creamy white sauce to accompany the roast beef I had ordered; I was pleased to discover that it was made with cren, the same root we love in my hometown, only prepared in a completely different way. Horseradish is relatively unknown in Brazil, except in the south, where I was raised. During the winter, my grandma would make a huge pot of broth with brisket, and after hours of boiling, she would skim the fat, remove the meat, and use this tasty clear broth to cook homemade soup with cappelletti—a stuffed pasta similar to tortellini. The leftover meat was tender, but it had a rich flavor. To cut the fattiness, we always ate it with a strong homemade vinegar combined with grated horseradish that had been left to cure for a few days. The boiled brisket paired with the vinegary horseradish was celebrated as much as the soup. I recommend this dish for Sunday supper on a cold day—it is very comforting, easy to make, and will fill the house with a gentle, steamy aroma. Plan ahead for making this dish, as the horseradish vinegar will need to be prepared one week in advance.

SERVES 8 TO 10

For the horseradish vinegar:

1 cup (230 g) freshly grated horseradish root or prepared white horseradish

1 cup (240 ml) good-quality strong red wine vinegar

For the boiled beef:

1 (2–3 lb) beef brisket, external fat completely removed, cut into 6 pieces

1 unpeeled yellow onion, halved

2 carrots, peeled and halved

1 leek, halved

4 cloves garlic, crushed

10 black peppercorns

2 tablespoons kosher salt

1 bunch Italian parsley

1 gallon (3.8 l) water

2 lb (900 g) Yukon potatoes, peeled

Finely chopped fresh chives, for serving

To make the horseradish vinegar, place the grated horseradish in a large Mason jar and cover with the red wine vinegar. (If you are using jarred horseradish, strain or squeeze out the excess liquid before using it.) Put the lid on the jar and let the horseradish steep for at least 5 days in the refrigerator. The horseradish vinegar can be kept in the refrigerator for up to 2 months.

To make the boiled beef, add the brisket, onion, carrots, leek, garlic, peppercorns, salt, and parsley to a large pot. Cover the beef and vegetables with water and bring to a boil. Reduce the heat to a gentle simmer and continue cooking for about 4 hours, occasionally adding more water if necessary. When the meat is tender to the point of shredding, add the potatoes and cook for another 15 minutes, or until the potatoes are tender. Transfer the meat, carrots, and potatoes to a serving dish and discard the remaining vegetables. Reserve the stock for other uses. Serve with the horseradish vinegar and chives.

After removing the beef, carrots, and potatoes, you can strain and use the remaining stock for cooking pasta or other dishes. The stock can be stored in the freezer for up to 4 months.

Pork Ribs with Yucca Flour

Costela de Porco com Farinha

This recipe has been in my family for a long time, and it is delicious and unique. In Brazil, it is common to eat ribs with farinha de mandioca (manioc flour) as a side dish, but in my family we cook the ribs with the farinha. When the pork ribs are almost done grilling, we coat them with farinha de mandioca and return them to the grill to make the farinha crispy. The farinha, which is very popular in Brazil, gets its flavor from absorbing all the fat and juices that would otherwise drip out and be lost. When cooked with the ribs over just the right fire, it adds a unique flavor and texture to the dish.

SERVES 4 TO 6

Salt

2 slabs St. Louis–style pork spare ribs

½ cup (120 ml) Texas de Brazil Marinade (page 71)

2 cups (145 g) coarse manioc flour (also known as cassava flour)

1 lime or lemon, halved

Pork ribs are not eaten with barbecue sauce in Brazil (actually, Brazilians don't eat *anything* with barbecue sauce), but since guests at Texas de Brazil in the United States usually request sauce with their ribs, we make an exception and serve them with sauce. All the other roasted meats served at Texas de Brazil are 100 percent authentic—from the marinades, to the seasoning, to the cooking techniques—exactly as it has been done in Rio Grande do Sul for centuries.

Apply salt to both sides of the ribs, and spread the marinade over the meat. Stack the ribs and let them rest to absorb the flavor for at least 2 hours in the refrigerator or, even better, overnight.

When ready to cook, prepare an outdoor grill with lump charcoal, and let it burn until the charcoals are glowing. Using 2 long skewers (1 per slab), skewer each slab by weaving the blade 2 to 3 times between the ribs so that each slab is secure on its skewer.

Place the skewers on the grill, about 12 inches (30 cm) from the charcoal, turning every 5 minutes until the meat is lightly brown and about 50 percent cooked (about 20 minutes). Remove the skewers from the grill and place them on a tray or sheet pan. At this point, the meat will still be moist on its exterior, so cover both sides of the ribs with the flour, making sure they are completely covered in order to form a nice crust. The exterior of the ribs must be moist so that the flour will adhere to the meat; if the meat is dry, the flour will not stick. If necessary, you can brush some melted butter or vegetable oil on the ribs to add moisture. Gently shake off any excess flour and return the ribs to the grill. The heat needs to be gentle; otherwise, the farinha will burn and the ribs will not be fully cooked and tender. It is very important to keep an eye on the ribs, moving and turning the skewer as needed. The ribs will be ready when a golden crust has formed, with some bubbling spots of fat. The meat should be tender. Using a set of tongs, remove the ribs from the fire. Place the slabs of ribs on a cutting board, remove the skewers, and cut between the bones into individual ribs. Squeeze some lime on top of the ribs and serve immediately.

Lamb Roasted on the Ground
Ovelha Assada no Chão

There are some very traditional and conservative gauchos who take their culture very seriously, to an almost religious level. For them, authentic churrasco is only beef or lamb, and the skewers—made from tree branches—must stand vertically directly in front of a fire on the ground. This is how the old ranchers would cook their meals during the long journeys away from home as they moved and traded cattle between different regions. Although I respect the gauchos' efforts to maintain a tradition that dates back centuries, I don't think that there is a single churrascaria in the world that could be considered authentic by this vigilant group. But I have to agree that the process of preparing and cooking a whole animal for several hours next to a fire built on the ground brings a lot of satisfaction.

I would be lying if I told you that this is the easiest way to cook a delicious lamb. But if you're curious or adventurous, you may want to try it for the experience or, like when I do it, to impress friends. I bought steel rods and some other metal parts from a home improvement store and got a friend to weld them for me. I use a four-armed cross spit (made of one long vertical rod and four shorter horizontal rods) to cook many things, from whole lamb and pigs to huge beef rib cages. It takes time to cook meat this way, but it is well worth the effort. (To create a spit for cooking meat, see page 84.) If you're feeling extra adventurous, you can also use this recipe to roast a whole goat or pig.

One final note: Refrain from undertaking this type of cooking when it's windy or when the temperature falls below 60°F.

In Rio Grande do Sul, we serve this lamb with bread and a simple green salad. We usually eat the meat right off the spit, with everyone taking a chunk of the meat with a knife. If you prefer, you can remove the lamb from the spit and serve it over butcher paper on a large table. Either way, this is a cooking and dining event that you and your guests are sure to remember!

SERVES 20

2 cups (280 g) kosher salt

18 cloves garlic, smashed

¼ cup (24 g) cumin

½ cup (55 g) white pepper

2 (12–16 oz/350–470 ml) cans light beer, or 4 cups red wine

1 bunch rosemary, chopped

1 bunch sage, chopped

1 bunch thyme or oregano, chopped

Large ice chest

Ice

Large sheet of plastic liner

1 whole young-lamb carcass (about 35 lb/16 kg)

40 lb (18 kg) firewood

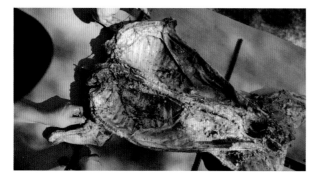
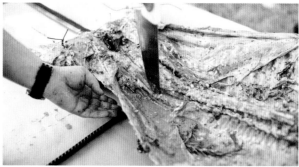

In a large bowl, mix the salt, garlic, cumin, pepper, and beer. Mix the rosemary, sage, and thyme in another bowl. Fill a large ice chest one-quarter of the way with ice, and cover the ice with the plastic sheet. Place the lamb on the plastic in the ice chest, and rub the meat with the beer mixture. Spread the herbs on all sides of the lamb. Fold the excess plastic over the lamb, close the lid, and let it marinate for about 2 hours (or refrigerate overnight if you have room).

When ready to cook the lamb, find a safe spot outdoors to build the fire. Make sure the spot you select is away from any structures or combustibles. Stack about one-third of the logs on the bare ground and use a fire-starter stick to light the fire.

While the wood starts to burn, lay a steel cross spit on a table. Lay the marinated lamb open over the spit. Using steel wire and a set of pliers, tie the bones from the front and rear legs onto the cross, then tie the spine to the center bar for extra support.

By now the fire will be burning nicely with moderate flames. With assistance, move the lamb in front of the fire, about 2 feet (60 cm) away, with the skin facing the heat. (If there is a moderate breeze, position the lamb so that the wind blows the heat toward the meat, not away.) Hammer the steel cross about 10 inches (25 cm) into the ground, or any depth necessary to ensure the spit is secure.

Cook the lamb for about 2 hours, adding more wood or moving wood away with a shovel to control the fire. You don't want the meat to cook too fast or start showing chars too early, since this is a slow cooking process. Once the skin is nicely golden, turn the spit to expose the other side to the fire and cook for another 30 to 60 minutes, depending on the amount of heat generated. Make a cut in the leg to check for desired doneness. If the meat needs more cooking, leave it on the fire a little longer and add more wood as needed.

Chicken Stew with Soft Polenta

Galinha com Polenta Mole

This comfort food was always present in our home. It came with the immigrants from the northern regions of Italy that settled in Rio Grande do Sul. Polenta, especially the fried version, has a very intimate connection with churrasco, and it is always served at roadside churrascarias in southern Brazil. This is a steamy and creamy variation of the classic peasant dish.

SERVES 6

For the chicken stew:

12 boneless, skinless chicken thighs

Salt

Freshly ground black pepper

1 sprig sage, chopped

1 sprig rosemary, chopped

6 tablespoons (90 ml) olive oil

6 cloves garlic

1 small yellow onion, finely diced

½ cup (120 ml) white wine

1 (14 oz/400 g) can good-quality crushed tomatoes

1 cup (240 ml) chicken stock

For the polenta:

4 ears white corn

4 cups (480 ml) water

2 tablespoons kosher salt

6 tablespoons (85 g) butter

1½ cups (240 g) finely ground cornmeal

1½ cup (170 g) shredded sharp white cheddar

1 cup (225 g) cottage cheese (optional)

Sharp cheddar shavings or Parmesan shavings

Chives, for garnish

To make the chicken stew, season the chicken with salt, pepper, sage, and rosemary. In a heavy-bottomed cast-iron skillet, heat the oil until it begins to smoke. Cook 6 pieces of chicken, turning once, until golden and nicely seared—they don't need to be fully cooked. Remove the first batch and cook the remaining 6 pieces of chicken, then set aside. Crush the garlic with the side of a knife, and add it to the skillet along with the onion. Cook over high heat. Once the onion is lightly golden, add the wine and the tomatoes and cook for about 3 minutes. Turn the burner to low heat, place the browned chicken over the sauce, add the chicken stock, and cook over low heat for 15 minutes. Taste the sauce and add salt if needed. Cook for another 45 minutes to 1 hour without stirring. If the sauce reduces too much, simply pour a small amount of water into the sauce at the side of the skillet as needed.

To make the polenta, shuck the corn and place the ears on the gas burner of the stove over a high flame to char them. (Skip the charring if you wish.) Use kitchen tongs to turn the ears so that they char evenly, making sure not to burn them. Remove the ears from the stove and allow to cool. Cut the kernels from the cob and reserve.

In a stockpot, bring the water to a simmer and add the salt and butter. Add the cornmeal slowly while whisking with a wire whisk. Cover and cook for about 20 minutes (up to 40 minutes depending on the quality of the cornmeal), stirring with a wooden spatula every 4 to 5 minutes. If the polenta becomes too thick, add a small amount of hot water and stir; if it is too runny, cook for a little longer, partially uncovered, until done. When the polenta has the consistency of porridge, turn off the heat and stir in the corn, cheddar, and cottage cheese. Season with salt if desired.

When serving, place about ½ cup of the creamy polenta, still very hot, onto a pasta plate and top with cheddar shavings. Place 2 pieces of chicken on top of the polenta, pour the tomato sauce over the chicken, and garnish with chives.

Brazilian Chicken Salad

Salpicão de Frango

When Americans think of salad, they usually think of something that's green and light in calories. For many Brazilians, when they think about salad, they think mayonnaise. A vegetable needs to be tossed with mayo to become an edible salad. In fact, Brazilians use mayonnaise with everything—we even spread it over pizza! In both cultures though, mayonnaise is a common ingredient in chicken salad, and this version is wonderful as an accompaniment for churrasco meats or on its own over a bed of crisp lettuce leaves.

SERVES 4 TO 6

2 qt (2 l) water

2 tablespoons salt, plus more for seasoning

1 lb (450 g) boneless, skinless chicken breasts, butterflied

½ medium white onion, cored and cut into matchsticks

½ cup (25 g) matchstick carrots

½ cup (46 g) thin green bell pepper strips

4 slices mozzarella, cut into strips

4 slices prosciutto cotto, cut into strips

12 European-style cornichons, cut into strips

1½ cups (330 g) mayonnaise

Lemon for garnish (optional)

Fresh cilantro for garnish (optional)

Fill a large pot with the water, add the salt, and bring to a boil. Place the chicken breasts in the water and simmer until cooked through, about 7 minutes. Remove the breasts from the pot and let them cool. In the same water, blanch the onion for about 3 minutes. Strain the onion and set aside to dry.

Once the breasts have reached room temperature, shred them by hand into thin strips. Season the carrots, onions, and bell peppers with a sprinkle of salt. Combine the chicken, carrots, onions, bell peppers, mozzarella, prosciutto, cornichons, and mayonnaise in a large bowl; stir gently. Place the bowl in the refrigerator to chill for at least 30 minutes. Garnish with lemon slices and cilantro before serving.

You can use more or less mayonnaise according to your taste. Mix 1 or 2 tablespoons of the cornichon brine with the mayonnaise to add a bright note to the salad. For added flavor and crunch, you can top each serving with a sprinkle of shoestring potato sticks.

Chicken Thighs with Beer

Sobrecoxa de Frango com Cerveja

For me, the chicken thigh is the most delicious part of the chicken; unlike the chicken breast, it is very hard to over-cook. I learned this recipe from my grandfather. It is a simple recipe, but you will be surprised by the amount of flavor it has. It was his favorite way of preparing chicken, and he would eat a dozen of them in one sitting. I remember eating almost as many as him, and my favorite part was—and still is—the crispy skin. Last year, while visiting an uncle in Brazil, I found the wooden bowl that my grandpa always used to marinate the chicken. I brought it home to my kitchen, and it fills me with wonderful memories every time I use it. You will need two skewers for grilling twelve thighs. Be sure that the skin is completely exposed to the fire so that it cooks to a crispy mahogany color. Then, perhaps, you will want to eat a dozen of them too.

SERVES 4

12 bone-in, skin-on chicken thighs

Salt and freshly ground white pepper

1 can (12–16 oz/350–470 ml) light beer

6 cloves garlic, minced

2 sprigs sage, chopped

2 sprigs fresh oregano

2 sprigs rosemary, chopped

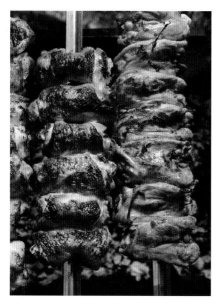

Rinse the chicken with cold water and pat dry with paper towels. Sprinkle both sides of the chicken with salt and white pepper. In a glass or stainless-steel bowl, mix the beer with the garlic, sage, oregano, and rosemary. Add the chicken thighs and toss lightly to cover all the pieces with the beer mixture. Cover the bowl and let the chicken marinate in the refrigerator for at least 12 hours.

Prepare a fire with lump charcoal as shown on page 53, letting the charcoal burn until all the pieces are glowing nicely. Remove the chicken from the refrigerator and drain all the liquid. Holding 1 piece of chicken at a time, fold the thigh to expose the skin, and cross the stainless-steel skewer just above the femur bone through the thigh and under the skin. Repeat the process until all of the chicken has been skewered.

Place the skewers on the grill, about 12 inches (30 cm) from the charcoal, and roast the chicken for about 30 minutes, turning the skewers every 2 to 3 minutes. If any char appears on the skin, the heat is too high, so move the charcoal to the side with a shovel or raise the chicken higher. The skin should have a uniform golden color, and when checking with a small knife, the meat around the bone should be fully cooked. Transfer the chicken to a platter and serve.

Try serving this dish with spaghetti and fried polenta.

Chicken Hearts
Coração de Frango

Chicken hearts are considered a delicacy in Brazil, and almost all churrascarias in the country offer them, even though the price of chicken hearts can be almost as much as the price of beef tenderloin. We had them on request when we opened our first restaurant, but our guests did not have the adventurous palates they now have, so we eventually stopped offering them. However, given the growing popularity for offal and the trend for restaurants to include more organ meat on their menus, this delicacy is not only worth including among the traditional churrasco recipes, but it's also worth a taste—you'll be pleasantly surprised.

There are many ways to prepare and use chicken hearts; in fact, some Brazilians even love them on pizza. The best way to prepare them is on skewers over an open flame. When made right, they will be a little chewy but delicious. Even picky kids enjoy eating them. Chicken hearts are never served as an entrée; they are served as a snack, often while sipping caipirinhas, to whet the appetite before the big feast begins.

SERVES 4 TO 6

2 lb (900 g) chicken hearts

1 cup (240 ml) white vinegar

4 tablespoons chopped fresh sage

4 tablespoons chopped fresh rosemary

2 tablespoons white pepper

¼ cup (34 g) kosher salt

8 cloves garlic, crushed

¼ cup (60 ml) vegetable oil

1 cup (240 ml) red wine or white wine

1 lemon, halved (optional)

In Brazil, chicken hearts are served with toasted cassava covering the bottom of the dish. The platter is passed around and guests serve themselves one or two at a time with a frilly toothpick—they are small enough to dispense with using a fork or knife.

With a small sharp knife, remove the fat and any outer membranes from the chicken hearts. Place the hearts in a colander and rinse with water. Transfer the cleaned hearts to a bowl, pour in the white vinegar, and toss with your hands. The vinegar will help release the blood inside of the hearts, resulting in a cleaner taste (a trick I learned from my father). Let the chicken hearts rest in the vinegar for 30 minutes, then drain them in a colander and discard the vinegar. Place the hearts back in the bowl and add the sage, rosemary, pepper, salt, garlic, oil, and wine. Squeeze the juice from the lemon halves over the hearts, then add the lemons to the mixture. Stir the ingredients together, cover the bowl, and let the hearts marinate for at least 2 hours or overnight in the refrigerator.

When ready to cook the hearts, heat up the grill. You will need 3 metal skewers to cook them. Pierce one-third of the hearts sideways onto the first skewer; repeat with the remaining hearts and skewers. Place the skewers on the grill over medium to high heat. Cook the hearts for about 15 minutes, turning every 5 minutes. The hearts should be fully cooked, with a slight char, but not dry. Use a pair of tongs to slide the chicken hearts onto a platter for serving.

Chicken "Drumstick" Fritter

Coxinha de Frango

This is a great savory snack molded to look like a chicken drumstick. Allegedly, this dish was created during the Brazilian monarchy era to satisfy the voracious appetite of a spoiled noble child for chicken drumsticks. When the cook for the royal family realized that she didn't have chicken legs, she shredded some leftover chicken, formed it into a drumstick-like fritter, and convinced the boy that it was a boneless drumstick. It worked so well that soon everyone in the court was eating them. Eventually, this snack became a favorite among the common folk. In many parts of Brazil, you can still find street boys carrying baskets of these coxinhas and selling them in front of office buildings or construction sites. Kids love them so much that they are always present at birthday parties. It requires a little practice to fold and fill the dough, but once you have done this a few times, it gets easier and quicker. The drumsticks also freeze well, so you can make an extra batch to defrost and serve for last-minute guests or as a weekend snack for the family.

MAKES ABOUT 18 FRITTERS

For the dough:

4 cups (960 ml) whole milk

1 tablespoon (15 g) butter

1 chicken bouillon cube, or 1 tablespoon chicken bouillon powder

Salt

4 cups (480 g) all-purpose flour

For the filling:

½ lb (230 g) boneless, skinless chicken breasts or thighs

Salt and freshly ground black pepper

2 tablespoons (30 ml) vegetable oil

½ small yellow onion, chopped

1 teaspoon minced garlic

1 small tomato, chopped

3 tablespoons chopped fresh Italian parsley

For the coating:

2 eggs

½ cup (120 ml) milk

2 cups breadcrumbs or Panko crumbs

Vegetable oil, for frying

To make the dough, add the milk, butter, and chicken bouillon to a large stockpot and bring to a boil over medium heat. It should taste like a creamy chicken broth. If necessary, increase the amount of bouillon and salt for balance and taste. Reduce to a low heat, slowly add the flour, and stir with a wire whisk for about 4 minutes. The dough is ready when it thickens and you can see the bottom of the pot when scraping it with a spatula. Transfer the dough to a pan or bowl, and keep it at room temperature until ready to use.

To make the filling, season the chicken pieces with salt and pepper. If the chicken breasts are very thick, cut them in half. Heat the 2 tablespoons oil in a sauté pan over medium heat, and sauté the chicken pieces until golden. Add the onion and garlic, cook for another 2 to 3 minutes, and add the chopped tomato. Season with salt and pepper. Reduce the heat to low and cook for about 15 minutes, stirring occasionally, then remove from the heat and allow to cool to room temperature. Remove the chicken pieces and shred the meat finely by hand. Add the chicken back to the sauce along with the parsley and stir, adding salt to taste.

To assemble the drumsticks, use your hands to form a golf-ball-sized amount of dough into a small pancake about ½ inch (13 mm) thick. Place 1 tablespoon of the chicken filling in the center of the dough and wrap tightly around the filling, forming it into the pear-like shape of a chicken drumstick. Repeat with the remaining dough and filling; set aside.

For the fritter coating, beat the eggs and milk in a bowl. Pour the breadcrumbs into a different bowl. Dip a fritter into the egg mixture, letting the excess drain back into the bowl, then roll it in the breadcrumbs, coating evenly. Repeat until all the fritters are coated. Heat 3 inches of oil to 350°F in a pot or electric fryer. Fry a few fritters at a time until the crumb coating turns golden brown. Remove the fritters from the oil and drain on paper towels before serving.

If freezing the fritters for future use, store after coating with breadcrumbs. Let the fritters defrost to room temperature before frying them.

Bucatini with Quail Sauce

Bucatini com Molho de Codorna

When the first Italian immigrants arrived in southern Brazil around 1875, they found an abundance of wildlife. Birds such as doves and partridges quickly became part of their diet. For many generations, hunting for partridges on cold foggy mornings was a tradition in my family. The preferred way to cook these not-necessarily-tender birds was slow-cooking them with tomatoes over a wood-burning stove to create a sauce that would be used to coat hearty, freshly made pasta dishes. Since partridges are difficult to find nowadays, quail is substituted in this delicious dish.

SERVES 6 TO 8

6 quails, halved

Salt and freshly ground white pepper

4 tablespoons (½ stick/60 g) unsalted butter

2 tablespoons (30 ml) olive oil

6 cloves garlic, chopped

1 sprig sage

1 small yellow onion, finely diced

1 tablespoon all-purpose flour

½ cup (120 ml) good-quality red wine (such as Merlot or Cabernet Sauvignon)

6 white mushrooms, finely chopped

1 (14 oz/400 g) can Italian crushed tomatoes

1 cup (240 ml) chicken stock or beef stock

1 lb (450 g) bucatini pasta (if necessary, substitute with spaghetti)

Grated Parmesan, for garnish

Pat the quail pieces dry with a paper towel, then season them generously with salt and white pepper. Melt the butter with the olive oil in a heavy-bottomed pan over medium to high heat. When the butter is almost smoking, arrange the quail in the pan so that the pieces do not overlap; depending on the size of your pan, you may need to cook the quail in batches. Cook for 3 to 4 minutes, turning occasionally, until the skin is golden; don't worry about undercooking, as the quails will finish cooking in the sauce. Remove the quails from the pan and set aside to rest. Add the chopped garlic and sage to the leftover juices in the frying pan. Once the garlic turns golden, add the onion and sprinkle the flour over the mixture. Stir for 1 minute, then add the wine, mushrooms, tomatoes, and stock. When the liquid comes to a low boil, return the quail to the pan. Reduce the heat to the lowest setting possible, cover the pan, and let the quail simmer gently in the sauce for about 1 hour. Scrape the bottom of the pan every 20 minutes or so, and add water if the sauce becomes too thick.

While the quail sauce is simmering, bring a large pot of water to boil and cook the bucatini according to the package directions. Drain the pasta well and transfer to a serving platter. Pour the quail sauce over the pasta and garnish with Parmesan.

Whole Fish Baked on a Roof Tile

Tainha na Telha

Tainha is a fish from the same family as the mullet and can be found all over Brazil. Many small towns hold annual festivals showcasing this fish and its unique preparation. The locals dig long, shallow ditches in which charcoal is placed and burned. Once the embers are ready, the fish is placed on roof tiles and cooked in the ditch. (These curved tiles are available at home improvement stores.) Many people believe the roof tile gives the dish a distinctive and earthy flavor. The presentation is dramatic, and the technique has some similarities to the way we prepare churrasco: it is a simple and rustic cooking method, it requires fire, and it allows you to drink and converse with friends while waiting for the fish to cook through. Here we will show you how to prepare the fish in the oven, but if you don't mind digging a ditch in your backyard, you can throw a party that your friends will remember for years to come. Since the tomato and onions in this dish form a very tasty sauce, it's usually eaten with boiled potatoes or white rice.

SERVES 4

4 unglazed clay roof tiles or unglazed terra-cotta tiles, long enough to hold each fish (alternatively, you can use a large clay cooking pot)

4 whole medium-sized red snappers, mullet, or branzinos, scaled and gutted Salt and freshly ground black pepper

1 sprig thyme or marjoram

2 small yellow onions, thinly sliced

4 tablespoons (56 g) minced garlic

4 medium tomatoes, seeded, crushed, and roughly chopped

½ cup (25 g) chopped scallions, white and green parts

2 tablespoons dried oregano

½ cup (120 ml) olive oil, divided

2 lemons, halved

4 tablespoons chopped fresh parsley

½ cup (90 g) capers, rinsed and dried

You will need 1 clay roof tile for each fish. Rinse the tiles very well but avoid using any soap.

Dry the tiles, place them in the oven, and heat the oven to 375°F for 10 minutes.

Season the interior of the fish with salt and pepper, place a sprig of thyme inside each fish, and set aside. Using oven mitts, remove the tiles from the oven and place side by side on a heatproof surface. Divide the ingredients in equal parts between the tiles in this order: onions, garlic, tomatoes, scallions, and oregano. Season the vegetables with salt and pepper.

Place 1 fish on top of each vegetable mix. Drizzle the fish with ¼ cup of the olive oil, and season the skin of the fish with more salt and pepper. Place the tiles back in the oven, and place a pan under the tiles to catch any running liquid. Bake the fish for about 25 minutes, until fully cooked but not dry.

Remove the tiles from the oven. Squeeze a lemon half over each fish, top with parsley and capers, and drizzle with the remaining ¼ cup olive oil. Serve the fish on the tile.

If you want to cook the fish over embers outdoors, you will need to find a safe place to dig a ditch and burn charcoal. Dig a long, straight ditch about 4 inches deep x 12 inches wide (10 x 30 cm) (or large enough to accommodate the amount of tiles you will be using). Spread about 10 pounds of charcoal in the ditch and light. Once the charcoal is glowing, place the tiles with the fish over the charcoal, and cover the tiles loosely with aluminum foil. Check the fish every 10 minutes until it is cooked and flaky.

Oven-Roasted Salted Cod
Bacalhau ao Forno

The Brazilians learned from the Portuguese to love bacalhau—salted, dried cod. There are countless family recipes for this dish, but most of them will have potatoes and traditional Portuguese items like olive oil and black olives. This recipe is my own interpretation that can be prepared in advance and finished in the oven just minutes before serving, making it a stress-free dish. Though the dish doesn't require any further accompaniments, it is still very refined. The best way to enjoy it is during a lunch outdoors on a hot Sunday with a chilled glass of white wine—even better if you can see the ocean from the table.

SERVES 4 TO 6

1 lb (450 g) salted codfish

1 cup (180 g) good-quality black olives, with pits

1 lb Yukon potatoes, peeled

1 cup (240 ml) olive oil

3 tablespoons (42 g) minced garlic

3 small yellow onions, thinly sliced

3 tablespoons capers

1 teaspoon freshly ground white pepper

1 teaspoon dried oregano

2 small tomatoes, thinly sliced

Salt

3 hard-boiled eggs, cut into ½ in (13 mm) slices

¼ cup (5 g) chopped fresh Italian parsley

Soak the codfish in warm water for about 1 hour, changing the water at least twice to reduce the saltiness of the fish. Meanwhile, break the olives into pieces by hand, discarding the pits, and then set them aside. Slice the potatoes ¼ inch (6 mm) thick. Transfer the potatoes to a pot, cover with water, and boil them just until tender but not breaking apart. Drain the potatoes and reserve.

Preheat the oven to 350°F.

In a small saucepan, heat the olive oil over medium heat and briefly sauté the garlic. Add the onions and cook until soft but not yet browned. Add the capers, white pepper, and oregano and stir. Turn the heat off and set the pan aside.

Arrange the sliced potatoes across the bottom of an 8 x 11-inch (20 x 28-cm) roasting pan. Remove the codfish from the water, draining any liquid from the fish by either squeezing gently or pressing between sheets of paper towel, and then break the fish into medium pieces. Spread the broken pieces of fish over the potatoes, arrange the sliced tomatoes over the fish, and lightly sprinkle the tomatoes with salt. Spread the eggs over the tomatoes, sprinkle with the parsley and the olives, and top with the onion and oil mixture, making sure to distribute the mixture evenly over the dish. Bake in the middle of the oven for about 20 minutes, or until the oil starts to bubble, being careful not to burn the onions. Serve immediately.

Codfish Fritters

Bolinho de Bacalhau

Codfish fritters are a real delicacy. Heavily salted, dried codfish from Portugal or Scandinavian countries is very expensive in Brazil and considered upscale. It's reserved for special occasions, especially around Easter, when most Catholics avoid eating red meat. Since the tips and trims of the salted cod are available at a lower cost, they are reserved to make the fritters. Bolinho de bacalhau is probably the most well-known comida de botequim, or tavern food. The botequim is an old institution in Brazil. It is a neighborhood pub visited exclusively by locals—mostly males—where the owner's family is usually in charge of cooking and serving unpretentious but tasty food, similar to Spanish tapas. I have visited several old botequims, and few places can match the character of these bohemian establishments. The spaces are small and the walls adorned with a few old and faded merchandise posters from tobacco and beer companies. The large doors are always open to a lazy street, and a few mismatching tables and chairs are spread along the sidewalk. The men's heated conversations revolving around football (soccer) and politics only stop when a beautiful woman passes by. Eventually, someone will pick up a cavaquinho (small guitar) and start playing a bossa nova song. Sometimes I dream of wearing my Havaianas (flip-flops) and meeting old friends at a botequim to play dominos and talk about life while savoring a platter of bolinho de bacalhau with an ice-cold beer on a warm afternoon.

MAKES ABOUT 16 FRITTERS

1 lb (450 g) salted codfish

Vegetable oil, for frying

1 lb (450 g) russet potatoes, peeled and boiled (unsalted)

2 tablespoons (30 ml) olive oil

2 tablespoons (14 g) minced garlic

¼ cup (13 g) finely chopped scallions, green and white parts

2 eggs, beaten

½ cup (15 g) finely chopped fresh Italian parsley

Freshly ground white pepper

Salt (optional)

Lime wedges, for serving

Soak the codfish in warm water for at least 5 hours, changing the water at least 3 times. After soaking, discard the water and squeeze the fish to release any moisture; discard any skin or bones and shred the fish finely by hand.

In a deep frying pan or electric fryer, heat 3 inches of oil to 350°F.

Pass the boiled potatoes through a potato ricer and into a large mixing bowl (or mash them well with fork). Add the shredded fish to the potatoes and mix well.

In a small sauté pan, heat the olive oil and sauté the garlic and scallions until garlic is fragrant and lightly golden (be careful not burn the garlic, or it will turn bitter); let the mixture cool. Pour the oil with scallions and garlic over the fish and potato mixture. Add the eggs, parsley, and white pepper; mix very well by hand. Taste the mixture and add salt if needed. Form the mixture into oval fritters about 2 ounces (60 grams) each. Drop the cod fritters into the fryer a few at a time, making sure they are completely covered in oil; fry until golden brown, about 5 minutes. Remove the fritters with a slotted spoon, and drain on a paper towel before serving. Serve with fresh lime wedges.

Cold Savory Torte
Torta Fria

In addition to churrasco, there are many other dishes that represent the customs of the gaucho people. Growing up in a large but close family, we had many birthday parties to attend, and all the mothers, including mine, would spend days in the kitchen preparing food for a party. When I look at old family photos, I can't believe the variety of dishes on the table—sweets, pastries, cakes, savories, and much more—all made by Mom and nicely arranged. The torta fria was one of everyone's favorites, kids and grown-ups alike. It is simply a huge sandwich that is decorated and served like a cake. To create this cake-like effect, it's best to visit a local bakery or gourmet shop that bakes and sells its own whole sandwich loaves and ask them to cut the loaf lengthwise, giving you long slices instead of the traditional short slices. You can mix and match whatever fillings you desire—chicken, ham, tuna, grilled vegetables, hard-boiled eggs, smoked salmon, etc.—with mayonnaise and spread them among the layers as if making a cake. You can even boost the flavor and color of the icing by adding chopped fresh herbs or ketchup to the mayonnaise.

SERVES 12

1 whole loaf white or wheat sandwich bread, sliced lengthwise

8 oz (225 g) cubed or sliced cooked chicken breast

2½ cups (550 g) mayonnaise

8 oz (225 g) mozzarella cubes or strips

10 small European-style cornichons

2 tablespoons (30 g) Dijon mustard

1 cup (50 g) matchstick carrots, blanched but not softened, finely chopped

Salt

1 (5 oz/142 g) can good-quality tuna in oil, drained, or 6 oz (170 g) deli ham

1 large tomato, peeled, seeded, and finely cubed (optional)

1 tablespoon smoked paprika, or a few threads saffron

2 tablespoons (30 ml) freshly squeezed lemon juice

Finely chopped fresh parsley, for garnish

Using a serrated knife, gently remove the bread's crust without smashing the bread. Discard the crust.

In a food processor, add the chicken with about ¾ cup of the mayonnaise, ½ cup of the mozzarella, 5 of the cornichons, and 1 tablespoon of the Dijon. Pulse the ingredients slowly to form a coarse paste. Transfer the mixture to a bowl, and fold in the carrots with a spatula. Season with salt to taste and set aside. In the same food processor bowl, pulse the remaining ½ cup mozzarella with the tuna, the remaining 5 cornichons, and ¾ cup of the mayonnaise until it reaches the same consistency as the chicken mixture. Transfer to another bowl, fold in the tomatoes with a spatula, and set aside. Both fillings should be moist enough to spread easily without making the bread soggy.

For the "icing" on the torta, mix the remaining 1 cup mayonnaise with the paprika and the lemon juice.

On a tray or cutting board large enough to accommodate the long slices of bread, lay the first slice and spread it with one-third of the chicken mixture. Top with another slice of bread and spread it with one-third of the tuna mixture. Repeat the process, alternating the fillings and making sure that there is a consistent amount in each layer. Top with a final slice of bread. The slices should be arranged so the sides are even and squared. You can use a serrated knife to trim the sides of the loaf to make it more uniform before icing. Using an icing knife or spatula, spread the icing mixture over the top and sides of the torta to cover completely to your preferred thickness. Sprinkle the fresh parsley on top. Let the torta rest in the refrigerator overnight to increase its flavor. When ready to serve, cut it into thick slices, like a cake or pie.

Squash Ravioli
Tortei de Moranga

If you go to the Serrana region of Rio Grande do Sul, you will find many restaurants called galeteria. The only meat served in these places is young chicken quarters, marinated in wine and herbs and spit-roasted over burning charcoal. The style of service in a galeteria is very similar to a churrascaria and almost as old. All the dishes are brought to the table family style, and they replace the dishes as many times as you desire for a fixed price per person, not per dish. Along with the delicious golden and crispy-skinned chicken, galeterias serve small tortellinis in a light chicken broth, green radicci salad, potato salad, fried polenta, and tortei de moranga, a delicious squash-filled ravioli that is largely cherished in that region.

SERVES 4 TO 6

For the filling:

4 tablespoons (½ stick/60 g) unsalted butter

12 ounces (340 g) ripe kabocha squash, peeled, seeded, and cut into ½ in (13 mm) cubes

2 tablespoons (11 g) grated Parmesan

1 teaspoon freshly ground nutmeg

Salt and freshly ground white pepper

For the dough:

3 cups (360 g) all-purpose flour

5 large eggs, beaten

1 tablespoon kosher salt

2 tablespoons (30 ml) olive oil

For the sauce:

6 fresh sage leaves

2 tablespoons (30 g) unsalted butter

1 shallot, diced

2 ounces (56 g) dried porcini mushrooms, or 1 cup chopped fresh wild mushrooms

1½ cups (350 ml) heavy cream

3 tablespoons (45 ml) brandy

Grated Parmesan, for garnish

Chopped fresh parsley, for garnish

To make the filling, melt the butter in a sauté pan, add the squash, and cook until soft, about 15 minutes. If the squash gets too watery, cook for a little longer. Transfer the squash to a plate and smash it using a fork, potato ricer, or potato masher; allow the squash to cool. Stir in the Parmesan and nutmeg, then season with salt and white pepper to taste. The filling must be firm, sticking to a spoon even if turned upside down. Reserve in the refrigerator until ready to use.

To make the dough, place the flour in a large bowl. Make a well in the center of the flour and add the beaten eggs, salt, and oil. Using your hands or a plastic spatula, mix until well combined. Transfer the dough to a lightly floured surface and knead until elastic and smooth, about 10 minutes. If necessary, add more flour to prevent the dough from sticking. Cover with plastic wrap and let rest for at least 30 minutes.

To make the sauce, tear the sage by hand into small pieces. In a sauté pan over medium heat, melt the butter and sauté the shallots, sage, and mushrooms until the shallots are soft and translucent. Add the cream and turn the heat to low. Add the brandy and cook the sauce gently until it reduces slightly. Remove from heat and set aside.

To assemble and cook the raviolis, bring a large stockpot of salted water to a boil. Divide the pasta dough into quarters. Using a pasta machine, form sheets of pasta $\frac{1}{16}$ inch (1.5 mm) thick. Cut the sheets into 4 x 4-inch (10 x 10-cm) squares. Place a dollop of filling in the middle of each pasta square and fold to form a triangle. Press the edges together gently to avoid air gaps, and seal the edges of the ravioli with your fingers. If the pasta is not sticking together well, use a small pastry brush to moisten the edges with water before resealing. Repeat the process to form more raviolis until you've used up the pasta and filling.

Add the raviolis to the pot of boiling water, reduce the heat to a simmer, and cook for about 3 minutes, until they start floating to the top and the pasta is al dente. Drain the raviolis and place them on a warmed serving platter. Cover with the sauce and sprinkle with Parmesan and parsley.

You can make extra raviolis and freeze them for later use. They will last in the freezer for about 3 months.

Spinach Cannelloni
Canelone de Espinafre

My mom used to make this dish for lunch once a week. Today, things are a little different in modern Brazil, but not many years ago, the whole family would have lunch together every day of the week. At noon, kids would leave school and dads would leave work to return home for lunch made by stay-at-home moms. The southern region of Brazil has a very strong Italian influence, and this dish, which is basically a round crepe stuffed with spinach and cheese, is similar to cannelloni. It can be also stuffed with cooked ground beef, ham and cheese, or other fillings. Even better, my mom would save some warm crepes so that my sister and I could spread them with a copious amount of doce de leite (see page 158) for the ultimate South American dessert.

SERVES 6 TO 8

For the crepes:

2 cups (475 ml) whole milk

1¼ cups (150 g) all-purpose flour

3 tablespoons (45 ml) vegetable oil, divided

1 egg

1 tablespoon kosher salt

For the filling:

3 (9 or 10 oz/255 g or 283 g) packages frozen spinach, defrosted

4 tablespoons (½ stick/60 g) salted butter

2 cloves garlic, minced

¾ cup (120 ml) heavy cream

1 cup (90 g) grated Parmesan plus more for garnish (about ½ cup)

1 cup (115 g) cream cheese, softened

Preheat the oven to 350°F.

To make the crepes, blend the milk, flour, 2 tablespoons of the oil, egg, and salt in an electric blender at medium speed for 30 seconds, making a silky batter. Preheat a 9- or 10-inch (23- or 25-cm) nonstick sauté pan over medium heat. (You can save time by working with 2 pans at the same time if you have them.) When the pan is hot, add a few drops of the remaining 1 tablespoon oil and spread it around with a folded paper towel. Pour a small amount of the batter—a little less than ¼ cup (60 ml)—into the pan, and rotate the pan in circles so that the batter covers the entire bottom. Cook for about 2 minutes; when bubbles start to form, gently turn the crepe over to cook on the other side. This is very similar to making pancakes, only these are thinner and lighter, with a golden color. Set the cooked crepe aside, and repeat the process until you have 6 to 8 crepes.

To make the filling, rinse the spinach and remove as much water as possible by squeezing the spinach with your hands or pressing it against the sides of a large strainer with the back of a spoon. In a large sauté pan over medium-high heat, melt the butter and cook the garlic until it is fragrant but not burned. Add the strained spinach and sauté for 3 to 4 minutes, until the spinach is cooked and no liquid is present. Stir in the heavy cream and cook for about 1 minute. Gently fold in the Parmesan and cream cheese and cook for 1 minute on low heat. Set aside.

On a clean work surface, lay 1 crepe flat and place 2 full tablespoons of the filling down the middle of the crepe, forming a line. Roll the crepe tightly, but avoid having the filling squeeze out of the open sides. Repeat the process until all the crepes are filled and rolled. You should have some creamed spinach leftover for serving.

Generously grease the bottom of a 10 x 15-inch (25 x 40-cm) glass baking dish. Arrange the crepes side by side in the dish. Place the crepes in the oven and cook for about 20 minutes, until the cheese begins to brown. Remove the crepes from the oven, garnish with Parmesan cheese, and serve the crepes individually over a bed of creamed spinach.

Collard Greens with Bacon
Couve com Toicinho

Gaucho cuisine is primarily meat based, so there are few vegetable dishes—and those are always simple. This one, also called couve a mineira *in many parts of the country, is one of the most popular—probably due to the addition of bacon and sausage—and it is a must-have accompaniment for many of the dishes in this book.*

SERVES 3 TO 4

3 bunches collard greens

¼ cup (60 ml) vegetable oil

6–8 thick slices bacon, diced

8 oz (230 g) kielbasa sausage, cut into ½-in (13-mm) slices (optional)

½ tablespoon minced garlic

Salt

Wash the collard greens, and remove the rib that runs down the back of each leaf with a paring knife. Stack about 6 leaves and firmly roll them into a cigar-like roll. Using a sharp chef's knife, slice the rolls into ½-inch (13-mm) slices. Repeat the process until all the leaves are rolled and sliced.

In a cast-iron pot over low to medium heat, add the oil, bacon, and sausage and cook gently, stirring occasionally. Once the sausage is cooked and the bacon is golden and crispy, add the garlic and cook for 1 minute. Add the collard greens and stir. Increase the heat to medium-high. Cook the greens for about 5 minutes, stirring and turning with a pair of kitchen tongs, until the liquid evaporates and the greens are slightly crispy. Turn off the heat and season with salt if desired.

In many parts of Brazil, beaten eggs are added to the collard greens at the end of the cooking process to create a delicious breakfast frittata.

Dandelion Greens with Bacon
Radicci com Toicinho

Gauchos love meat above everything else, but they do know that salads are healthy for you. In my hometown, everyone shares a passion for a special salad: radicci com toicinho, a dish that I have never seen in any other part of the world. Radicci is a small and bitter green leaf that you will not find in the United States, but it is somewhat comparable to dandelion greens (or pissa cane, as my grandfather used to call them), another traditional green in the Serra Gaúcha region. The greens are healthy and the bacon provides flavor. This is a great salad to serve with a roasted chicken and a robust red wine on a cold winter night.

SERVES 4

1 lb (450 g) bacon slab, cut into ¼-in (6-mm) cubes

2 bunches young dandelion greens

⅓ cup (80 ml) good-quality red wine vinegar

Salt

Cook the cubed bacon over medium heat in a heavy skillet that is compact enough for the bacon to be partially submerged in its own fat as it cooks. Wash the dandelion greens and pat dry between paper towels. Arrange them in a shallow salad bowl or on a tray.

When the bacon is golden brown and crispy and about ¾ cup of fat is rendered, add the red wine vinegar slowly to avoid grease splashes. Stir briefly to deglaze the pan and dislodge any bits of bacon stuck to the skillet. Pour the bacon/vinegar mixture over the dandelions, season with salt, and serve promptly.

This salad should be served immediately after dressing, so if your main dish is not ready or the table is not set, keep the bacon mixture on a low heat until ready to dress and serve the greens.

Fried Polenta Stuffed with Cheese

Polenta Frita Recheada com Queijo

When I was a child, my grandma would tell me how difficult it was when her family emigrated from Bassano del Grappa, Italy to Rio Grande do Sul, the southernmost state of Brazil. Food was extremely scarce, and for a very long time, polenta was the only thing readily available to eat. Even as conditions—and life in general—improved, polenta remained a staple on everyone's dinner table in the Serra Gaúcha (Gaucho Highlands). I never cared for the soft version of polenta made simply by boiling cornmeal in water; it was too bland, almost tasteless. But when leftover polenta gets cold, it hardens and can then be cut into sticks and fried in hot oil or lard—now that's a magical transformation. When stuffed with cheese, it becomes a side dish or snack that you may find difficult to stop eating. This polenta is also a great accompaniment for pan-fried sausage.

SERVES 6 AS A SNACK OR SIDE DISH

3 cups (700 ml) water

1½ cup (240 g) cornmeal

2 tablespoons salt

Vegetable oil, for frying

4 oz (113 g) mozzarella, cut into ½ x 3-in (13 mm x 7.5-cm) sticks and then frozen

In a pot, bring the water to a boil, then slowly stir in the cornmeal with a wire whisk to break up any lumps. Add the salt and keep stirring until the polenta thickens and then bubbles. Reduce the heat to a gentle simmer and cook for about 30 minutes, stirring every few minutes. The final consistency should be like a thick yogurt, forming peaks when you raise the wire whisk. If the mixture gets too thick, add water and stir; if it is too watery, continue cooking until thickened. Once ready, pour the polenta into a glass or metal baking pan, to make a 3 inch (7.5 cm) high layer. Let it cool completely, preferably overnight in the refrigerator, until very firm. After the polenta is fully chilled, place a cutting board on top of the pan and flip both upside down to remove the polenta. Cut the polenta into sticks about 4 inches long x 1½ inch wide (10 x 3.5 cm).

In a heavy saucepan or fryer, heat 3 inches of oil until it reaches 350°F. Fry a few sticks at a time until golden, firm, and crispy, about 7 minutes. Drain the fried sticks on a paper towel, and continue frying the remaining polenta sticks until they are all cooked. While you fry the next batch, insert a stick of frozen cheese into a stick of just-fried polenta (with the help of a pair of tongs or a kitchen towel to prevent burning your hands)—the warm polenta stick will melt the cheese. Repeat with remaining polenta until all the snacks are fried and filled with cheese. Serve warm.

Seasoned Cassava Flour
Farofa Gaucha

Farinha de mandioca is very popular in all regions of Brazil and many parts of Africa. It is made by grinding the cassava root (yucca), drying it, and sometimes toasting it. In its original form, the farinha is very bland, but Brazilians love to use it as a condiment, dipping fatty pieces of meat in it to give it a crusty texture and make the overall meal feel healthier. However, once you add a few ingredients to the farinha de mandioca you have a different dish called farofa. While there are numerous variations on this dish—and I've never met two Brazilians who could agree on what makes a good farofa—this particular recipe is flavorful and satisfying to most of them.

MAKES 5 CUPS (1 L)

½ cup (1 stick/240 g) unsalted butter

6 slices bacon, chopped

2 small shallots, thinly sliced

4 tablespoons (56 g) minced garlic

4 large eggs, beaten

½ lb (230 g) coarse manioc (cassava) flour, preferably toasted

¼ cup (25 g) kalamata olives, drained, pitted, and chopped

¼ cup (40 g) raisins or dried cranberries

½ cup (25 g) chopped scallions, green and white parts

Salt

Heat the butter in a sauté pan and cook the bacon until crispy. Add the shallots and garlic, and stir until golden. Pour the beaten eggs over the bacon mixture and cook until the edges are crispy and lightly browned. With a wooden spatula, break the eggs into small pieces. Add the flour and mix for 2 minutes. Turn off the heat and mix in the remaining ingredients until blended. Season to taste with salt.

Wagoners' Rice
Arroz Carreteiro

This dish dates back to the 1800s. A carreteiro was a person who transported goods, supplies, and other items in an oxcart across southern Brazil. Since refrigeration had yet to be developed, these old-time gauchos would always carry plenty of salted, charque (dried beef), which they often used to prepare a simple yet satisfying rice dish during their long journeys. Nowadays, gauchos are notorious for overestimating the quantity of beef needed for a weekend churrasco, and we always cook much more meat than we can possibly eat. As a result, this dish remains popular, since it makes good use of all the leftovers. There are many versions of this recipe, but this is my own.

SERVES 6 TO 8

4 cups (760 g) uncooked jasmine rice or parboiled rice

2 thick slices bacon, chopped or cubed

3 tablespoons (45 ml) olive oil

4 cups (approximately ½ kilo) chopped or cubed leftover grilled beef, preferably with some char marks and fat (dried beef can also be used)

4 cloves garlic, smashed

1 medium onion, chopped

½ cup chopped green onions, green and white parts

Dash of crushed red pepper

1–2 cubes beef bouillon

6 cups hot water, plus more as needed

Salt

Fresh Italian parsley, chopped, for garnish

Grated Parmesan, for garnish

If using jasmine rice, prior to cooking, rinse the dry rice with water in a mixing bowl, straining the water until it runs clear to remove any excessive starch. Drain well and reserve.

Render the bacon in the oil in a 4- to 6-quart cast-iron pot or Dutch oven over medium-high heat until golden brown. Add the beef, garlic, and onion, and sauté for 2 minutes, stirring constantly. Stir in the rice and sauté for 2 minutes, then add green onions, red pepper, beef bouillon, and water; add salt if needed. Bring to a boil and then reduce the heat to low. Cover and simmer for about 20 minutes, or until the rice has absorbed the water. If the water has been completely absorbed but the rice is still undercooked, add a bit more water and allow it to cook a little longer.

When the rice is cooked, turn off the heat and gently stir it with a spoon so that all the ingredients are well mixed. Cover the pot with a clean kitchen towel and let it rest for 2 to 3 minutes. Just before serving, garnish the rice with the parsley and Parmesan.

If you remove the lid and allow the rice to cook for 5 to 7 minutes at a low temperature, the bottom of the rice will form a nice crust that is extremely flavorful. To create the crust without burning the dish, it is imperative to use a heavy cast-iron pot.

Cattlemen's Beans

Feijão Tropeiro

Tropeiros were the men that would trade and move cattle from one place to another. Because of this nomadic life-style, the tropeiros carried limited food supplies—and beans were nutritious, filling, and easy to cart. The beans were used to create a rich and robust dish that could be cooked quickly in a skillet over a fire during rest stops to ease hunger and boost energy. The original Feijão Tropeiro consisted of leftover beans cooked the day before with some sausage or dried beef and farofa. This is a more modernized recipe, but the main ingredients and techniques are the same, including the use of leftover beans—you'll prepare them a day ahead of time. There is something very comforting about a dish that starts with bacon and sausage cooked on a cast-iron skillet—the aromas fill the room like few other dishes can.

SERVES 4 TO 6

1 lb (230 g) dried pinto beans

Salt

6 tablespoons (90 ml) vegetable oil or pork lard

5–7 slices bacon, cut into small pieces

1 lb (230 g) kielbasa-style pork sausage, halved and cut into ½-in (13-mm) pieces

3 tablespoons (42 g) minced garlic

1 medium yellow onion, diced

4–5 malagueta peppers, smashed and chopped, or 1 jalapeño, diced

4 stalks scallions, diced

1 cup (120 g) coarse manioc (cassava) flour

4 tablespoons chopped fresh parsley

Soak the beans in cold water for about 2 hours, or overnight, adding more water if the beans absorb the water and become dry. Transfer the beans and water to a 4-quart stockpot, and add more water to cover the beans by about 1 inch. Cover the pot and cook the beans over a medium-low heat for about 1 ½ hours, until the beans are soft and a thick sauce has formed. Season to taste with salt. Transfer the beans and sauce to a container, and refrigerate overnight.

To prepare the dish, pour the oil into a heavy cast-iron skillet, and cook the bacon and sausage over medium-high heat. Once the bacon has browned, add the garlic, onion, peppers, and scallions, and cook for about 3 minutes. Add the flour, stir the mixture for 1 minute, and then add the cooked beans. Stir well and cook for another 2 to 3 minutes. The mixture will be thick and compact. Cook uncovered and uninterrupted for about 10 minutes over low heat. After this, turn the heat to high and cook for another 1 to 2 minutes to form a nice crust on the bottom and sides of the skillet. Turn the skillet upside down over a large serving plate and serve immediately.

For a complete meal, serve the Feijão Tropeiro with a fried egg and a green salad simply dressed with vinegar and oil.

Brazilian Vinaigrette

Vinagrete/Molho Campeiro

Vinagrete in Brazil is not a salad dressing, but more of a salsa-like condiment that is usually served in churrascarias. Brazilians from the south usually prefer their beef cooked medium to medium rare, while those from central and northern Brazil tend to like their beef well done. This salsa goes well with any doneness, but it can save an over-cooked steak by giving it much-needed juiciness. This vinagrete, known in Brazil as molho campeiro, is to Brazilians what chimichurri sauce is to Argentinians. Like chimichurri, there are regional variations in the way it is prepared, but it always starts with ripe tomatoes. This recipe is delicious with any churrasco-style meat, especially flap steak.

MAKES ABOUT 3 CUPS (700 ML)

2 large ripe tomatoes

½ white onion, cut into ⅛-in (3-mm) cubes

¼ cup (45 g) diced green bell pepper (⅛-in [3-mm] cubes)

¼ cup (45 g) diced yellow bell pepper (⅛-in [3-mm] cubes)

½ cup (120 ml) water

½ cup (120 ml) white vinegar

½ cup (120 ml) vegetable oil

1 tablespoon kosher salt

3 tablespoons chopped fresh Italian parsley

1 tablespoon dried oregano

Freshly cracked black pepper

With a sharp knife, quarter the tomatoes. Scoop out the seeds and juice and reserve. Cut the tomato quarters into small cubes, about ⅛ inch (3 mm)—the tomatoes, onion, and peppers should all be diced to the same size for a unified presentation. In a mixing bowl, add the water, vinegar, oil, reserved tomato juice with seeds, and salt; whisk briefly with a fork. Add the diced vegetables, parsley, and oregano and season to taste with salt and pepper. Cover and chill in the refrigerator for 1 hour so the flavors can meld. The vinaigrette be kept in the refrigerator for up to 2 days.

Chocolate Truffles
Brigadeiro

One of the most popular chocolate desserts in Brazil is the brigadeiro, a buttery chocolate bonbon with the texture of a thick ganache and covered with chocolate sprinkles. It is the Brazilian version of the chocolate truffle. Perhaps the most interesting thing about this treat is that it is always served at children's birthday parties. And because Brazilians usually attend many birthday parties during their childhood, there's a sentimental connection to the brigadeiro that lasts a lifetime. It is a true comfort food that's not only served at home, but is also available at bakeries and fancy restaurants around the country. The recipe is much simpler to make than you might think and the results are delicious.

SERVES 18 TO 20

1 (14 oz/400 g) can sweetened condensed milk

6 oz (170 g) good-quality dark cocoa powder

2 tablespoons (30 g) unsalted butter

Chocolate sprinkles

Mix the condensed milk, cocoa powder, and butter together in a heavy-bottomed saucepan. Cook the mixture on low heat, stirring continuously with a wooden spoon for about 15 minutes. When you start to see the bottom of the pan as you scrape the mixture with the spoon, it's ready. Be careful—if overcooked, the mixture will crystallize; if you remove it from heat too soon, it will become gluey.

Remove the mixture from the heat and let it cool completely. Using your hands, form the mixture into small balls approximately 1½ inches (38 mm) in diameter. Pour the chocolate sprinkles onto a plate and gently roll the balls in the sprinkles until completely covered. Serve the bonbons in small paper baking cups. The chocolates can be kept in the refrigerator for 1 week; just remove them 1 hour before serving and bring to room temperature.

Dulce de Leche/Caramelized Milk

Doce de Leite

This is a silky, caramel-like jam of milk that is sweet and decadent. As kids, we would call it Mu-Mu (Moo-Moo), because of the dominant manufactured brand that could be found in every grocery store in my hometown. Like the yerba mate and other culinary traditions, this treat brings the Brazilian gauchos closer to Argentina and Uruguay, where the equivalent—dulce de leche—reigns supreme. Dulce de leche is used for almost all dessert creations, from ice creams to cakes to alfajores (cookies filled with it). In most households, it is always on the table for breakfast to be spread over bread. I have tried dulce de leche in many parts of South America, but nothing compares to the product found in Argentina, Uruguay, and south Brazil; this is due to the high quality—and high fat content—of the cow's milk produced in the region. If you can find unpasteurized, fresh milk for this recipe, that's great. Otherwise, you can use organic whole milk. One of my favorite ways to enjoy doce de leite is with warm crepes (see page 140), but I always keep a jar of this sweet delicacy in my refrigerator to take a spoonful at any time.

MAKES 2 CUPS (475 ML)

½ gal (3.8 l) organic whole milk

1 pinch kosher salt

3 cups (600 g) sugar

1 teaspoon baking soda

In a large 4-quart saucepan with a heavy bottom, mix the milk, salt, and sugar over medium heat. Bring to a gentle boil and use a wooden spoon to stir until the sugar is well dissolved. Add the baking soda and stir for another 1 minute or so. Reduce the heat to a low simmer and cook uncovered for about 2½ hours. Stir the mixture every 10 to 15 minutes, scraping the bottom of the saucepan.

The doce de leite will be ready when the mixture thickens and turns a deep caramel color. Remove from the heat and let cool. Transfer the doce de leite to 1 or 2 jars and keep it refrigerated for up to 1 month.

TEXAS DE BRAZIL FAVORITES

Gaucho-Style Beef Ribs
Costela Gaucha, 162

Garlic Picanha
Picanha no Alho, 165

Spit-Roasted Flap Meat
Churrasco de Fraldinha, 166

Parmesan-Crusted Pork Loin
Lombinho de Porco com Queijo, 169

Pork and Black Bean Stew
Feijoada, 170

Roasted Leg of Lamb
Pernil de Ovelha, 172

Texas de Brazil Lamb Chops
Chuletinha de Ovelha, 175

Bacon-Wrapped Chicken Breasts
Peito de Frango com Toicinho, 176

Garlic Shrimp Salad
Salada de Camarão com Alho, 179

Lobster Bisque
Creme de Lagosta, 180

Coconut Fish Stew
Moqueca de Peixe com Coco, 183

Cream of Jalapeño Soup
Creme de Jalapenho, 184

Bulgur Wheat Salad
Tabbouleh, 187

Texas de Brazil Potato Salad
Salada de Batata, 188

Potato Au Gratin
Batata Gratinada, 191

Fried Bananas with Cinnamon
Banana Frita com Canela, 192

Caramel Flan
Pudim de Caramelo, 194

Sautéed Mushrooms with Wine Sauce
Cogumelos ao Molho de Vinho, 197

Brazilian Cheese Bread
Pão de Queijo, 198

Papaya Cream
Crème de Papaia, 201

The Brazilian Caipirinha
Texas de Brazil Classic Caipirinha, 204

Strawberry Caipirinha with Mint
Caipirinha de Morango e Menta, 205

Gaucho-Style Beef Ribs
Costela Gaucha

For many gauchos, this is the most traditional cut of churrasco. When you look at vintage photos of old gauchos roasting meats on long spears next to a ground fire, you will notice a large rack of ribs nearby, and there is no traditional wedding celebration without the costela gaucha. Recently, many towns in south Brazil, Argentina, and Uruguay have been competing to break the record for the "Biggest Churrasco in the World" by cooking thousands of whole rib cages at once. Records aside, I can assure you that there are few more exciting things in this world than being part of the Festival da Costela (beef ribs festival)—the light smoke and incredible aroma in the air is a meat lover's dream. Gauchos and meat lovers can argue about which cut is the most flavorful to cook churrasco style, but they will all agree that no cut smells as good over a wood fire as beef ribs.

Gauchos don't care much for tender beef ribs—they actually prefer them fatty and a little chewy. In the Pampas they use their adagas (daggers) to cut large chunks of meat directly from the ribs and eat it one piece at the time, right next to the fire. At Texas de Brazil, we prefer to cook the ribs a very long time until they are tender. The smoke from the burning wood of our grills adds a wonderful flavor to the meat, but it can be replicated in your own oven with great results.

SERVES 6 TO 8

1 slab (8 lb/3.5 kg) short plate beef ribs, (3–4 bones)

½ cup (70 g) kosher salt

¾ cup (180 ml) warm water

To create a richer flavor, replace the water with ½ cup (120 ml) red wine and add 2 finely diced shallots and 1 tablespoon of minced garlic about 20 minutes before removing the ribs from the oven.

Preheat the oven to 375°F.

Place the beef ribs bone side down on a cutting board. Trim the fat on top to about ½ inch (13 mm), and rub the kosher salt into the top fat area only—not the sides. Using a folded paper towel or your fingers, gently brush off any loose salt, but make sure to leave a crust of it adhered to the fat cap.

Place the ribs in a large roasting pan and transfer to the oven. Bake for about 35 minutes, or until the cap of fat achieves a deep golden color. Add the warm water to the bottom of the pan and reduce the oven temperature to 275°F. Bake for another 1½ to 2 hours. The water will evaporate completely, and the meat should be very tender. Transfer the ribs to a serving platter or tray.

The fat rendered from the ribs is great for roasting potatoes. When the ribs are about 30 minutes from being ready, remove the roasting pan from the oven and add 1 pound (450 g) unpeeled potatoes that have been parboiled in salted water. Toss the potatoes gently in the liquid fat, then place the roasting pan back in the oven to finish cooking the ribs and potatoes.

A Note about Plate Ribs

Plate ribs vary in fat cap content: some are trimmed very well, while others have a large amount of fat on them. When buying the meat, avoid plate ribs that are completely trimmed of fat—the meat will become dry and have too little flavor. If the plate ribs have too much fat, trim it down to about ½ inch (13 mm), but make sure all areas of the meat are still covered with fat. This might seem like a lot of fat, but it will melt into a salty, perfectly golden, and delicious layer.

Garlic Picanha
Picanha no Alho

This is a true delicacy for garlic lovers and one of the most requested cuts at Texas de Brazil. This menu item was created to utilize the trimmings of the picanha. As for the garlic element, many churrascarias in Brazil simply add minced garlic to the tips of raw picanha and skewer the meat to be grilled later. I find the flavor to be too strong and pungent—the meat will turn a slight green color and all you can taste is the garlic. As a subtle alternative, I decided to create a simple garlic sauce to brush over the meat just seconds before grilling—the result was amazing. It strikes the right balance between meat and seasoning, and the garlic flavor is milder and more pleasant.

SERVES 6 TO 8

½ cup (60 g) garlic cloves

½ cup (120 ml) vegetable oil, divided

1 (2½ lb/1 kg) picanha

Kosher salt

In a blender, add the garlic and ¼ cup (60 ml) of the oil. Cover and blend at medium speed for about 5 seconds. Remove the lid carefully, and with the blender on a low setting, slowly add the remaining ¼ cup vegetable oil. Blend until the oil emulsifies and the sauce has the consistency of mayonnaise, about 20 seconds. Be careful not to overblend or the sauce will break. Transfer the sauce to a small container and refrigerate. This can be prepared 1 day in advance.

Prepare the grill with about 10 pounds (4.5 kg) of lump charcoal (see page 53).

Place the picanha on a cutting board. Use a sharp knife to remove excessive fat and create a uniform cap about ¼ to ½ inch (6 to 13 mm) thick. Turn the meat over and remove any silver skin and connective tissue from the bottom. Cut the picanha against the grain into 1¼-inch-thick (3-cm) strips. Cut the strips into 3-inch-long (7.5-cm) slices.

Using the end of a skewer, pierce the center of the meat and slide it onto the skewer. Repeat this until all the meat is centered between the handle and the end of the skewer. Once all the meat is on the skewer, sprinkle with kosher salt and use a pastry brush to apply the garlic paste. Apply as much you want, but remember that a little goes a long way.

Place the skewer on the grill, about 12 inches away from the charcoal. Cook for about 8 minutes over high heat, or until the meat chars and the garlic turns a dark golden color. Turn the skewer over and repeat. When done, move the skewer to a moderately heated section of the grill, and let it rest for 5 minutes. Transfer the pieces of meat to a heated platter and serve.

Spit-Roasted Flap Meat
Churrasco de Fraldinha

This is the second most popular cut of meat served at Texas de Brazil, and it is not uncommon to have guests asking our carvers to bring nothing else but flap meat to their tables. While not the most tender cut of beef, its robust and delicious beefy flavor completely makes up for the lack of tenderness. There is much confusion surrounding this cut—many people mistake it for skirt steak, flank steak, or hanger steak. All of these cuts have similar textures and flavor, but the correct name of the cut we serve is flap meat or sirloin flap (see page 61 for more about flap meat). Since the name "flap meat" doesn't sound very appealing, we sometimes call it "flank steak" when offering it to the table. The truth is that we buy and cook flap meat because it is a superior cut. Flap meat is thicker than skirt or flank steak and much larger than hanger steak. It is derived from the bottom sirloin butt, very close to the picanha, whereas flank steak is cut from the bottom of the short loin portion of the steer.

We have different standards for the aging of our beef. Some of the cuts, like tenderloin, need very little aging. Flap meat, however, needs thirty to forty-five days of wet aging before cooking; otherwise, it will be extremely chewy and difficult to eat. Many of our other cuts of meat are prepared with various seasonings and marinades. However, when it comes to flap meat, we prefer this simple cooking technique, using only coarse kosher salt as seasoning.

This cut is ideal for churrasco-style cooking—the extreme temperature that our grills can reach is perfect for cooking flap meat. It needs a lot of dry heat to cook properly, and it absorbs the smokiness of the hardwood charcoal more than any other cut. It is crucial to leave some fat on the meat, as the fat will melt away and add a lot of flavor while cooking. I wouldn't attempt to grill flap meat that was completely stripped of its external fat. Procure your meat from a reputable butcher that can guarantee quality, then follow this recipe. You will be serving a meat as good as any served in a first-class churrascaria.

SERVES 10

5 lb (2.2 kg) flap meat (wet-aged for at least 30 days)

⅓ cup (45 g) kosher salt

Prepare the grill with about 15 pounds (6.8 kg) of lump charcoal (see page 53).

Trim most of the visible silver skin from the meat. Carefully trim only the thickest areas of fat (in most cases there is no need to remove any fat).

Lay the meat down flat on a cutting board, insert the tip of the skewer into one of the ends of the flap meat, and slowly guide the tip of the skewer through the center of the meat until it crosses the meat completely. Generously season the thicker areas with the kosher salt and season lightly on the thinner areas and edges.

When the charcoals are glowing and showing some white ashes, place the skewer about 10 inches above the charcoal. Roast the steak for 10 to 12 minutes, then turn the skewer and roast the other side for another 10 to 12 minutes. When both sides are brown and show moderate to intense charring, use a knife to make a small cut to reveal the center of the meat. If you prefer it more well done, take it back to the grill and let it cook until desired doneness is reached. If you are satisfied with the doneness of the meat, move the skewer to a cooler section of the grill and let it rest. Resting time is recommended for many cuts of beef, but for flap meat it is a must. The optimum rest time is at least 15 minutes in order to retain the natural juices and increase tenderness. The meat can rest on the grill as long it is placed in an area of low heat. When ready to serve, lay the meat on a cutting board and remove the skewer. Using a sharp knife, slice the meat thinly and always against the grain.

Add an extra layer of flavor to the flap steak by infusing the salt with garlic and rosemary. Simply smash about 4 cloves of garlic until it turns into a paste, chop a sprig of rosemary very thin, and mix these together with the salt. Let the flavors infuse for a day or two before using.

Parmesan-Crusted Pork Loin

Lombinho de Porco com Queijo

Another classic churrasco dish is lombinho com queijo, which is a must in any Brazilian restaurant. If you think pork is bland, this preparation is sure to change your mind. The marinade, herbs, and cheese combine to create a wonderful burst of flavor.

SERVES 6 TO 8

1 (2 lb/900 g) center-cut pork loin

3 tablespoons kosher salt

1 cup (240 ml) Texas de Brazil marinade (page 71)

6 fresh sage leaves, finely chopped

1 sprig rosemary, finely chopped

¾ cup (65 g) grated Parmesan, plus more for garnish

Place the pork loin on a cutting board. Without removing any of the fat, cut the pork into 1-inch-thick (2.5-cm) slices, then cut each slice into 4 or 5 strips. Season the meat with the kosher salt and transfer to a mixing bowl. Pour the marinade over the pork, mix well, cover, and refrigerate for at least 4 hours, or overnight.

Prepare the grill with about 10 pounds (4.5 kg) of lump charcoal (see page 53).

While the grill is heating, skewer the pork—the fat side of the meat should be facing outwards so that it will render and brown nicely while cooking. When all the pork pieces are skewered, sprinkle them evenly with sage and rosemary. Place the skewers on the grill, about 12 inches (30 cm) from the charcoal. Cook for about 15 minutes, turning the skewers every minute or so. The pork should be mostly cooked but still moist.

Transfer the skewers to a baking sheet and sprinkle all sides of the pork with the Parmesan. Return the skewers to the grill and cook for about 3 minutes, turning a few times, just until the cheese begins to warm—this keeps the meat from drying out. If you prefer your meat more well done, cook the pork until the Parmesan melts and turns crispy and lightly golden, but be careful not to overcook. With the help of tongs, transfer the pieces of meat to a serving platter and sprinkle with additional Parmesan.

Pork and Black Bean Stew
Feijoada

This is, without a doubt, the national dish of Brazil. Churrascarias may be Brazil's largest contribution to the international culinary scene, but feijoada is the dish that is enjoyed by Brazilians from every region. Arroz e feijão—rice and beans—are staples in the Brazilian diet, as well as many other Latin American countries. For many families, the traditional lunch consists of rice, black beans, meat, and a vegetable. The daily beans and rice dish is simple: black beans slow cooked for a couple of hours with onions, garlic, seasonings, and meat, usually smoked pork. This preparation is typically called feijão. Feijoada, however, is more complex and delicious. Its history goes back to the nineteenth century, when plantation owners would slaughter pigs and keep the premium cuts for their families. The tail, skin, nose, feet, and other parts were given to the workers, mostly slaves, who were living on the plantation's grounds. To make those parts edible, the slaves would stew them with black beans and a few seasonings in large caldrons for several hours. It didn't take long for the plantation owners to notice that feijoada was a wonderful dish, and it was soon served on the owners' tables. Feijoada has evolved over the years, and adding smoked meats is now a must. There are even restaurants in Brazil that serve feijoada exclusively and for a fixed price, like churrascarias. Diners can sample all the meats and sausages used in its preparation since they are placed individually in clay pots, along with the traditional accompaniments: white rice, collard greens, torresmo (cracklings or chicharrónes—crispy pig meat and fat), orange segments, and farofa.

We never considered serving the real feijoada at Texas de Brazil, because, while offal is gaining in popularity among those with adventurous tastes, many of our regular customers might not appreciate finding a pig nose or tail on their plate. The recipe we use contains many of the main ingredients, yet it is still as rich and delicious as the traditional. The ham hock is optional, but it will add a lot of flavor.

SERVES 6

3 cups (680 g) dried black beans

1 lb (450 g) beef (such as skirt steak or sirloin), cut into 1-inch cubes

Salt

2 tablespoons (25 g) pork lard, or ¼ cup (60 ml) vegetable oil

6 oz (170 g) smoked bacon, cut into small pieces

1 small yellow onion, diced

½ bunch scallions, thinly sliced, green and white parts

8 cloves garlic, smashed

8 oz (230 g) smoked kielbasa sausage or Brazilian Paio sausage, cut into 1½ in (38 mm) pieces

½ lb smoked pork ribs (optional)

1 smoked ham hock (optional)

2 dried bay leaves

2 small hot peppers (such as malagueta), or 1 small jalapeño, seeded and sliced

Steamed white rice, for serving

Collard Greens with Bacon (page 142), for serving

Wash the beans under running water and set aside. Season the cubed beef generously with salt and set aside.

In an 8-quart (8 l) Dutch oven over medium heat, cook the lard and bacon until bacon is golden brown. Add the onion, scallions, and garlic and stir constantly until cooked through. Turn the heat up to high and add the sausage and the beef. Cook for about 5 minutes, stirring often, until the meat is brown. Add the beans, ribs, ham hock, bay leaves, and hot peppers and stir together. Add enough water to cover the mixture by 2 inches (5 cm). Bring to a low boil, then cover the pot and lower the heat to a simmer. Cook the stew for about 2 hours. During cooking, the beans will absorb most of the liquid, so add more water whenever the liquid covering the beans is less than ½ inch. The dish will be ready once the beans have softened and the stew thickens and turns mahogany brown. The beef should retain its shape. Taste the stew after 1 hour of cooking and add salt if needed. Serve over steamed white rice with a side of Couve Com Toicinho (collard greens with bacon).

Roasted Leg of Lamb

Pernil de Ovelha

Some time ago, our lamb supplier confided that Texas de Brazil—and churrascarias in general—have done more for the lamb business in the United States than any other type of restaurant. And he was correct. If you dine at a traditional steakhouse, there is a good chance that lamb chops will be on the menu, but since they are usually expensive, the majority of diners prefer to play it safe and order a beef cut like filet mignon or rib eye. In a churrascaria, however, guests have the opportunity to try several different varieties and cuts of meat; they will always try the lamb—and they love it. Many of our guests have admitted that it had been "an eternity" since they had ordered lamb, and that they didn't remember how good it could be. They recall lamb being mostly gamy and without much taste, but not so with the lamb we serve.

A whole leg of lamb roasted over an open flame will make a satisfying meal for you and your family and make a great impression on your guests.

MAKES 8 TO 10 SERVINGS

1 (5 lb/2.3 kg) semi-boneless leg of lamb

¼ cup (34 g) kosher salt

¾ cup (180 ml) Texas de Brazil marinade (page 71)

2 sprigs rosemary

12 cloves garlic, minced

Oven-roasted potatoes or mashed potatoes for serving

Place the leg of lamb on a cutting board. Place the tip of a chef's knife next to the femur (thigh bone) and push the knife down, parallel to the bone—this creates a cavity inside the leg that will hold the marinade and salt. Rub the kosher salt generously all over the leg and inside the cavity. Pour the marinade over the lamb and spread it with your fingers so that the meat is covered and the marinade enters the cavity. Cover the lamb in plastic wrap and allow to marinate in the refrigerator for at least 4 hours, but preferably overnight.

When ready to cook, prepare the grill with lump charcoal (see page 53).

While the charcoal is heating, skewer the lamb with a heavy stainless-steel skewer, starting from the shank end and crossing through the leg.

Chop the rosemary and mix it with the garlic by smashing both with the side of a large knife—this will form a paste. Spread this paste all over the lamb, then transfer the skewered meat to the fire, about 18 inches from the heat. Cook for about 1 hour over medium heat. The lamb will be ready when the outside achieves a beautiful dark-gold color—the rosemary and specks of perfectly golden garlic should be visible—and the interior of the lamb is about 140°F. The meat around the bone in the middle of the leg should be pink in color, not red (undercooked) or gray (overcooked). Transfer the meat to a serving platter or cutting board, and let it rest for 15 minutes before carving. Serve with a side of oven-roasted or mashed potatoes.

If you are cooking the lamb with other meats, keep in mind that it takes much longer to cook a whole leg than it does smaller cuts. Plan the cooking time of each meat in advance so that all the cuts will be done at the same time.

Texas de Brazil Lamb Chops

Chuletinha de Ovelha

For me, there are few things better than medium-rare lamb chops—well seasoned, with the fat melted just right, and with tasty spots of char. This is not a cut of meat that gauchos traditionally prepared —it was too fancy and expensive— but as diners' tastes grew broader and more sophisticated, upscale churrascarias began to serve them. Now, lamb chops are one of the most popular items at Texas de Brazil. Quality matters, so we buy the best lamb we can find directly from ranches where the animals are raised free range on a pasture diet and without antibiotics. When preparing this dish, buy your lamb chops at a local butcher, farmer's market, or upscale organic food market; choose racks with a minimum weight of 18 ounces for about eight chops. Using high-quality meat with this simple preparation will result in a savory and satisfying meal.

SERVES 4

2 Frenched racks lamb (with fat cap)

2–3 tablespoons kosher salt

4 tablespoons (½ stick/60 g) unsalted butter, softened

4 tablespoons (48 g) good-quality lemon pepper seasoning

Prepare the grill with lump charcoal (see page 53), letting it burn completely until the embers are glowing.

Cut the rack between the bones to form single-bone chops—each rack will give you 8 to 9 chops. Place the chops on a work surface and season them with kosher salt on both sides. Brush a small amount of butter on both sides of the meat, then season generously with the lemon pepper seasoning.

Place a clean oiled grate over the fire and let it become very hot. Using a pair of tongs, place the chops over the grate. Watch them carefully as they cook—the fat will melt and the chops will form char marks very quickly, so remove promptly to achieve a perfect medium rare. Transfer the chops to a serving plate and enjoy.

To make the rack easier to cut into chops, chill the meat in the freezer beforehand. The best way to serve these chops is medium rare, but if the chops are thin and it takes too long for them to form a nice char, they will become well done. To avoid that, make sure the temperature of the grill is extremely hot.

Bacon-Wrapped Chicken Breasts

Peito de Frango com Toicinho

There is a reason why Texas de Brazil and most churrascarias in the United States and Brazil don't serve plain chicken breast: when cooked alone, the white meat may dry out and lack the flavor to compete with more savory cuts like picanha or lamb chops. So churrascarias wrap chicken breasts with bacon—this helps the poultry retain its juiciness and adds a smoky flavor.

SERVES 6 TO 8

⅓ cup (80 ml) freshly squeezed lemon juice

1 cup (240 ml) red wine

⅓ cup (80 ml) olive oil

1 tablespoon chopped fresh thyme

½ tablespoon chopped fresh rosemary

⅛ teaspoon ground cumin

2 lb (900 g) boneless, skinless chicken breast, cut into 16 (2-oz/56-g) cubes

1½ tablespoons kosher salt

16 thin slices bacon (preferably applewood-smoked)

16 fresh sage leaves

Freshly cracked black pepper

Create a marinade by combining the lemon juice and wine in a large mixing bowl. Slowly stir in the oil with a wire whisk. Mix in the thyme, rosemary, and cumin. Season the chicken with salt, place it in the marinade, and refrigerate for at least 1 hour, or as long as overnight.

Prepare the grill by burning lump charcoal as shown on page 53.

Lay the bacon slices flat on a clean surface, and put a cube of marinated chicken on top of each slice. Place a sage leaf on top of each chicken cube, and wrap the chicken with the bacon. Sprinkle with cracked pepper. Slide 8 bacon-wrapped chicken cubes onto each skewer, making sure the pieces of chicken are placed slightly apart so that the bacon will cook evenly. Place the skewers on the grill and cook, turning the skewers frequently, until bacon is crispy and charred and the chicken is cooked through but not dry, about 15 minutes. Transfer to a plate and serve.

Garlic Shrimp Salad

Salada de Camarão com Alho

Seafood doesn't have a place next to a skewer of picanha or a leg of lamb on the gaucho grill. Don't get me wrong—I love seafood. But a real gaucho reveres the tradition of churrasco too much to have land and sea side-by-side over the same fire. However, this doesn't prevent many churrascarias from offering a large selection of seafood in their salad areas, including shrimp salad and even sushi. It is, in fact, a must in almost every churrascaria in Brazil today. I came across this shrimp recipe at a small tapas bar in Madrid, and I loved how the smoked paprika and the garlic worked with the warm shrimp. I enjoyed it so much that I adapted the recipe for our own kitchens.

SERVES 4

½ cup (120 ml) olive oil

6 tablespoons finely chopped garlic

½ cup (120 ml) white vinegar

3½ tablespoons salt, divided

1–1½ lb (450–680 g) large shrimp (preferably wild-caught gulf shrimp or black tiger shrimp), peeled and deveined

1 tablespoon (15 ml) freshly squeezed lemon juice

1 tablespoon (15 ml) Tabasco sauce

1 small jalapeño, thinly sliced

2 tablespoons Spanish smoked paprika

2 tablespoons chopped fresh parsley

Pour the oil into a small sauté pan over medium heat. When the oil is hot, add the garlic and stir constantly for 3 to 5 minutes, until the garlic is golden and crispy but not burnt. Remove the pan from the heat, and immediately transfer the garlic and oil mixture to a bowl to stop the cooking process. Let it cool at room temperature.

In a stockpot, bring 4 to 6 quarts (4 to 6 l) of water to just below boiling. Add the vinegar, 3 tablespoons of the salt, and the shrimp. Cook for about 5 minutes, without boiling, until the shrimp are opaque. Drain the shrimp well, but do not run cold water over them or use ice—the shrimp should be dry to the touch. Transfer to a mixing bowl and season the warm shrimp with the remaining ½ tablespoon salt. Add the lemon juice, Tabasco, and jalapeño and toss well. Pour the garlic and oil mixture over the shrimp and toss. Add the smoked paprika and fresh herbs and toss again gently. Transfer the shrimp to a serving platter. It can be served cold or room temperature, but it is best when served warm.

Add firm white fish, scallops, or calamari to make a complete seafood salad.

Lobster Bisque
Creme de Lagosta

Although churrascarias in Brazil rarely serve soup, we decided that it would be a great addition to our menu, so we served a different soup every day of the week for many years. One cold winter day, our food supplier left behind a box of lobster shells by mistake, so we roasted them with some vegetables and added cream. After we served the lobster bisque that night, we had guests calling to find out when we would serve the bisque again so they could book a reservation. That's when we realized we should make it part of our daily menu.

Lobster bisque is a French specialty, but we keep this recipe rich, complex, and slightly spicy—without masking the sweetness of the lobster—with a touch of brandy and a pinch of cayenne. This is a wonderful dish to warm you up on a cold night or to whet your appetite for a meaty main course.

MAKES 10 TO 12 CUPS

For the roux:

1 cup (120 g) all-purpose flour

¾ cup (1½ stick/170 g) unsalted butter, softened

For the bisque:

1 small yellow onion

2 large carrots

1 small red bell pepper

4 stalks celery

4–6 lobster shells, or 2 medium cooked lobsters (fresh or frozen)

1 tablespoon minced garlic

1 tablespoon sugar

¼ cup (55 g) tomato paste

½ lb (4 sticks/230 g) unsalted butter, softened

Salt

6 cups (1.4 l) water

Pinch of cayenne pepper

1 sprig tarragon

8 cups (1.9 l) heavy cream

½ cup (120 ml) brandy

Cooked lobster meat, for garnish

Finely chopped fresh chives, for garnish

Preheat the oven to 350°F. Thaw the lobster if using frozen. Prepare the roux by mixing the flour and butter together in a heavy-bottomed 10-inch (25 cm) pan. Cook at medium heat for about 10 minutes, stirring constantly with a wooden spatula, until the roux turns medium beige in color and emits an aroma similar to toasted nuts. (Be careful not to overcook or burn the roux.) Remove from heat and allow to cool.

Chop the onion, carrots, pepper, and celery into small pieces and set aside.

If using whole lobsters, remove all the meat and save for garnishing or for another recipe. Place the lobster shells between 2 clean kitchen towels, and use a rolling pin or the side of a small frying pan to break the shells into pieces that are 2 inches (5 cm) or smaller—the more you break the shell, the more flavor you will extract. Place the shells into a heavy roasting pan, approximately 10 x 12 inches (25 x 30 cm), and roast in the oven for about 10 minutes, or until the shells turn pink. Remove the pan from the oven and add the chopped vegetables, garlic, sugar, tomato paste, and butter. Sprinkle with salt and continue roasting in the oven for 25 minutes, or until the edges of the vegetables show some light charring.

Transfer the ingredients from the roasting pan to a 2-gallon (7.5-liter) stockpot. Add the water, cayenne pepper, and tarragon and simmer for 30 minutes uncovered. Using a fine mesh strainer over a bowl or container large enough to collect the liquid, strain the contents of the pot. Use the back of a ladle to press the solids and extract as much liquid as possible. Remove any pieces of lobster meat and reserve. Discard the shells and transfer the strained stock back to the pot.

Over moderate heat, bring the stock to a simmer. While stirring with a wire whisk, slowly add the roux 1 tablespoon at a time until blended. Add the heavy cream and brandy and raise the temperature slightly, just below boiling, stirring constantly for about 2 minutes to heat through. Add a touch of salt to taste.

Serve the bisque in warm soup bowls and garnish with the reserved lobster meat and fresh chives.

Coconut Fish Stew
Moqueca de Peixe com Coco

This is a fish dish that we only serve in select locations or on special occasions. It is very popular in the northern parts of Brazil, where fish is a dietary staple and coconut is largely available. We have many northern Brazilians visiting our churrascarias, and they are always happy when this seasonal dish is served. Azeite de dendê—oil from a palm tree—is essential in the cuisine from Bahia. It gives a lovely golden color to the dish, and I highly recommend using it if you can find it. There is some flexibility when it comes to the seafood in this recipe: you can use any white fish (such as cod), and you can select shrimp of any size, which can be left whole or peeled and deveined as desired. Like paella, this dish can be cooked and served in the skillet. If desired, the dish can be accompanied by white rice or boiled potatoes.

SERVES 6

1 tablespoon (15 g) unsalted butter, or 2 tablespoons (30 ml) palm oil

⅓ cup (80 ml) olive oil, divided

6 (6–8 oz/170–230 g) fillets white fish (about 1 in/2.5 cm thick)

½ lb (230 g) whole, unpeeled shrimp

Salt and freshly ground white pepper

¼ cup (30 g) all-purpose flour

1 tablespoon minced garlic

1 large yellow onion, cut into ¼ in-thick (6 mm) slices, divided

3 bell peppers (preferably 1 yellow, 1 red, and 1 green), cut into ¼ in (6 mm) strips, divided

2 ripe tomatoes, peeled, seeded, and chopped

Juice of 2 lemons

1 bunch cilantro, chopped, divided

1 (14 oz/400 ml) can unsweetened coconut milk

Preheat the oven to 425°F.

In an ovenproof skillet, heat the butter and half of the olive oil over medium heat. Season the fish and shrimp with salt and white pepper, then dredge both sides of the fish with flour. When the butter and oil mixture is hot, fry the fish fillets 2 or 3 at a time for about 3 minutes per side, just enough to cook the exterior and give it some color. Transfer the fish to a plate and set aside.

In the same skillet, sauté the garlic, shrimp, and half of the onions for about 2 minutes. Add half of the peppers and sauté for 1 minute. Add the chopped tomatoes and stir. Turn off the heat and return the cooked fish (along with its juices) to the skillet. Pour the lemon juice over the fish and shrimp, then sprinkle with half of the chopped cilantro. Stir the coconut milk with a fork and pour over the seafood. Place the remaining raw peppers and onions on top of the seafood, season with salt and white pepper, and drizzle with the remaining olive oil. Transfer the skillet to the hot oven and cook for about 15 minutes, or until the fish and vegetables are cooked through and the coconut milk starts to bubble. Before serving, sprinkle with the remaining cilantro.

Cream of Jalapeño Soup
Creme de Jalapenho

Believe it or not, you can grow tired of eating picanha and beef ribs every day! At the restaurant, it is customary for our entire staff to eat the same meats and salads we serve to our guests. But once in a while, our cooks want something different, so they will take what is available in the kitchen and create a completely different meal. When I visited one of our restaurants in Texas, the cooks offered me some soup they were eating after the lunch service. At first I thought it was the cream of asparagus that we sometimes serve on the lunch menu, but when I ate the first spoonful, I was amazed by the wonderful spicy flavor—it was cream of jalapeño. I told the chef to serve the soup on the lunch menu. We began receiving emails asking for the recipe from the very first day it was served. The soup is simple to make, but the number of jalapeños needed for a batch can vary depending on the heat of the individual peppers. Sometimes it takes only six or seven peppers to make a full batch of soup, while other times it can take two dozen to achieve the same heat. Start with a few jalapeños and taste the soup as it cooks to achieve the desired level of spiciness.

SERVES 4 TO 6

1 tablespoon (15 ml) vegetable oil

3 large jalapeños, halved and seeded (add more if the peppers are not very hot)

1 small ripe tomato, quartered

4 cloves garlic

1 bunch cilantro

½ cup (120 ml) water

4 tablespoons (½ stick/60 g) butter

1 small onion, finely diced

1 cube chicken bouillon, or 1 tablespoon chicken bouillon powder

4 cups (950 ml) heavy cream

Salt

Sliced bread, toasted

Heat the oil in a small sauté pan over high heat. Add the jalapeños, tomato, and garlic and cook for about 2 minutes, or until the skin of the jalapeños show some blisters and slightly darkens in color. Transfer the sautéed jalapeño mixture to an electric blender. Add the cilantro and water, blend thoroughly at medium speed, and reserve.

In a stockpot, melt the butter and cook the onion until soft. Add the chicken bouillon, the blended jalapeño mixture, and the cream to the pot. Stir well and add salt to taste. Cook gently, without fully boiling, for about 5 minutes and serve with toasted bread.

Bulgur Wheat Salad
Tabbouleh

You may wonder why tabbouleh—one of the most traditional Middle Eastern salads—is noted here in a book about gaucho cuisine. When the first churrascarias started spreading from Rio Grande do Sul to São Paulo, the owners soon realized that they would be able to attract a larger clientele by offering a few dishes that were popular in that region. São Paulo has a large Arab community, particularly Lebanese, so adding tabbouleh to the salad bar seemed the right thing to do. Many of the churrascarias in São Paulo also started offering kibbeh as an appetizer before the parade of meats. Since that time, tabbouleh has become a must-have salad at most churrascarias around the world, and the one we serve at Texas de Brazil is especially delicious.

SERVES 8

1 cup (140 g) fine-grain (#1) bulgur wheat, soaked overnight in 3 cups (700 ml) water

1 cup (240 ml) olive oil

⅓ cup (80 ml) freshly squeezed lemon juice

2 bunches Italian parsley, stems removed, finely chopped

1 cup (200 g) diced tomato (with juice and seeds)

½ cup (70 g) finely diced white onion

2 tablespoons finely chopped mint leaves

Salt

Strain the water from the bulgur and squeeze it well to remove any excess liquid. Transfer the bulgur to a large bowl, add the oil and lemon juice, and mix well with a silicone spatula. Gently mix in the parsley, tomatoes, onion, and mint and season with salt. Taste and add more salt, lemon juice, or oil if needed. The tabbouleh can be served immediately, though many people believe it tastes better when chilled overnight and served the next day.

Texas de Brazil Potato Salad

Salada de Batata

Any gaucho would be disappointed if a churrasco meal didn't include potato salad. There are countless interpretations of this classic dish, including many family recipes. In my family, and the majority of other gaucho families, men have always been in charge of the churrasco, and women have always been in charge of the potato salad. This unusual recipe, featuring hearts of palm, has been in my family for many years. In my opinion, this is the best potato salad you will ever try. Yukon potatoes work best for this salad because they are creamier in consistency than other varieties. As for the hearts of palm, try to find a Brazilian brand that is packaged in a glass jar. Most importantly, the distinct flavor of this salad comes from the cornichon brine, which tends to be vinegary. Since each brand of cornichons has a different degree of saltiness and acidity, opt for European style. However, you must work carefully with the brine—if you use it too sparsely, the salad will lack flavor, but using too much will make it taste too tart. Strive to keep the flavor balanced.

SERVES 8 TO 10

3 lb (1.5 kg) Yukon potatoes, peeled

½ (14 fl oz/400 g) jar hearts of palm, drained

2 cups (440 g) mayonnaise

½ cup (120 ml) cornichon brine (the juice from a jar of cornichons, preferably European style)

Salt

4 tablespoons chopped fresh parsley, chives, or cornichons, for garnish

Bring a large pot of salted water to a boil. Cut any large potatoes in half before boiling. Boil the potatoes for about 20 minutes, or until very tender—almost falling apart. Drain the water and let the potatoes cool at room temperature (do not refrigerate).

Meanwhile, thinly slice the hearts of palm. In a medium bowl, mix together the mayonnaise, hearts of palm, and cornichon brine.

Once the potatoes are cool enough to be handled, but still relatively warm, chop into irregular medium-sized pieces—not too thin but not large chunks. Place the potatoes in a large bowl. Gently fold in the mayonnaise mixture with a silicone spatula. Season to taste with salt. Transfer to a serving dish and refrigerate for about 1 hour, or until ready to serve. Garnish with parsley, chives, or cornichons just before serving.

It is important to let the potatoes cool at room temperature. If you try to refrigerate the potatoes to speed up the cooling process, a film will form over the potatoes that will prevent them from properly absorbing the mayonnaise dressing.

Potato Au Gratin

Batata Gratinada

Most "gratin" dishes are baked in the oven, but our potatoes are made in a saucepan and finished in the oven to form a nice crust. We must be doing something right because this is not only one of our most popular dishes, but it's also one that garners the most recipe requests. Though we've served this side dish for a long time, it has become much more popular since I decided to add an ample amount of brandy to the sauce, so do not skimp on adding it. At Texas de Brazil, the dish is served without spinach, but you can add it here to create a complete meal.

SERVES 6 TO 8

1 (10 oz/283 g) package frozen spinach (optional)

¾ cup (1½ stick/170 g) butter

6 cloves garlic, minced

2 shallots, finely diced

2 cups (475 ml) heavy cream

2 cups (180 g) grated Parmesan, plus more for garnish (about ⅓ cup)

⅓ cup (80 ml) brandy

Vegetable oil, for frying

2 lb (900 g) small Russet potatoes

Salt

Chopped fresh parsley, for garnish

Defrost the spinach, squeeze it by hand to rid it of excess moisture, and set aside.

Preheat the oven to 375°F.

Melt the butter in a saucepan over medium heat. Add the garlic and shallots, and cook until soft. Add the cream and reduce the heat to low. When the cream begins to lightly simmer, immediately add the Parmesan. Whisk the cream and cheese constantly for about 4 minutes, keeping it at a low simmer. Add the brandy and stir until blended. Remove from the heat and cover to keep the sauce warm. The cheese sauce can be made up to 3 days in advance and refrigerated until ready to use.

Heat 3 inches of oil in a fryer or large pot to 350°F. Using a mandoline, cut the potatoes into about ¼-inch (6-mm) slices; discard the ends. Deep-fry the potatoes in the hot oil until fully cooked and lightly colored—they don't need to be crispy. Transfer the potatoes to a paper towel to drain and sprinkle with salt.

Transfer the spinach and about three-quarters of the cream sauce to a mixing bowl; fold together gently. Fold in the fried potatoes while they are still hot. Transfer the potatoes to a round skillet (about 4 inches deep) or a small roasting pan. Using your hands, arrange the potato slices evenly for a nicer presentation. Pour the remaining sauce over the potatoes, and then sprinkle the Parmesan on top. Bake for about 10 minutes, or until the cheese melts and turns golden in color. Remove from the oven, garnish with parsley, and serve immediately.

Fried Bananas with Cinnamon
Banana Frita com Canela

Every table at the restaurant is served a plate of this sweet treat just before the meat service begins; it works well as a palate cleanser between servings of different meats. This dish can also be served with vanilla ice cream for a delicious ending to a meal. For best results, make sure the bananas have the right degree of ripeness: they should be firm and just beginning to turn yellow.

SERVES 4 TO 6

1 cup (200 g) sugar

¼ cup (30 g) confectioners' sugar

1 tablespoon ground cinnamon

Vegetable oil, for frying

6 firm bananas

Mix the sugars and cinnamon in a wide bowl or plate.

Pour 2 inches (5 cm) of oil into a large, heavy-bottomed pot or deep-fryer, leaving at least 2 inches (5 cm) between the oil and the top of the pot. Heat the oil over medium heat until it reaches 350°F.

Peel the bananas. Fry 2 to 3 bananas at a time until they turn a deep golden color, about 5 minutes. Remove the bananas from the pot with a slotted spoon and transfer to the plate with the sugar mixture. Once fried, the surface of the banana will be dry to the touch, not soggy, and the interior will be tender. With the assistance of a spoon, gently roll the fried bananas in the sugar mixture, making sure that they are completely coated. Transfer the bananas to a serving plate, keeping as much of the sugar on the bananas as possible. Repeat the process with the remaining bananas and serve.

If you want your bananas to have the same golden-colored syrup as the ones from Texas de Brazil, let the fried and coated bananas rest in a 140°F oven or food warmer for about 10 minutes. This will allow the sugar to melt and form the delicious syrup.

Caramel Flan
Pudim de Caramelo

Flan is one of our best-selling desserts. Originating in Europe centuries ago, it has been adopted by many Latin countries as a traditional dessert, and I cannot imagine a churrascaria in Brazil or elsewhere not including it on the menu. There are many variations of this classic, but at Texas de Brazil we serve the traditional version that I grew up with. The ingredients are few, but they should be high quality. Using organic whole milk and fresh cage-free eggs with orange yolks will make all the difference.

It is a simple dessert to make, but the key to its success is the caramel—the sweetness of the custard and the light bitterness of the caramel should marry perfectly. Burn it and the dessert is ruined; undercook it and you will have sugar syrup, not caramel, making the dessert unbearably sweet. Since sugar is inexpensive, you might want to make a test batch or two.

At restaurants, flan is prepared and served in individual ramekins, but at home it is cooked in a glass Bundt pan. That might seem like a lot of flan, but you'll find it goes quickly with everyone wanting a second helping.

SERVES 12

6 large eggs

2 (14 oz/400 g) cans sweetened condensed milk

3½ cups (830 ml) whole milk (preferably organic)

1½ cups (300 g) sugar

½ cup (120 ml) water

Preheat the oven to 275°F. In a blender, add the eggs, condensed milk, and whole milk. Blend at medium speed for 30 seconds and reserve. *Note:* If your blender is not large enough to hold all of the ingredients in one batch (50 fluid ounces/1.5 l), then blend in two batches.

In a small saucepan, mix the sugar and water with a silicone spatula and cook over low to medium heat for about 20 minutes, or until the mixture turns a dark amber color similar to honey or maple syrup. Stir just a few times and very briefly—avoid stirring too often. Keep a close eye on the sugar mixture when it starts to turn a light amber color because it will darken quickly. If you find it difficult to see the actual color of the caramel while it's in the pan (as it often looks darker than it actually is), spoon a small amount of the caramel onto a white dish or into a clear glass. The caramel will continue cooking even when the saucepan is removed from the stove, so work fast or it will turn dark and bitter.

Transfer the caramel sauce to a heatproof glass or metal Bundt pan about 10 inches wide x 3 inches deep (25 x 7.6 cm), and immediately swirl the pan so that the sauce will stick evenly to all sides. This layer of sauce should not be very thick; if the pan has too much sauce, tilt the pan over the sink to remove any excess. Let the caramel set for 10 minutes.

Before baking the flan, you will need to prepare a water bath. Place the caramel-lined Bundt pan in a deep baking pan or roasting pan, and fill the pan with warm water until it reaches almost halfway up the glass pan. Gently add the flan batter to the Bundt pan. Transfer the pans to the oven and bake for about 1 hour. The flan should be set, but still a bit wobbly. (You can check by shaking the pan gently.) Remove the Bundt pan from the oven, let it cool at room temperature for 1 hour, and then refrigerate for at least 4 hours.

When ready to serve, carefully turn the flan out onto a serving platter. Use a silicone spatula to scrape the caramel sauce from the sides of the Bundt pan and pour over the flan before serving.

Variations:

ESPRESSO FLAN

Espresso is a great complement to the caramel flavor of the flan. Simply add 1 shot of strongly brewed espresso to the blender along with the milk and eggs.

COCONUT FLAN

After you spread the caramel sauce inside the Bundt pan, sprinkle 1 cup (75 g) of shredded sweetened coconut in the bottom of the pan before pouring in the custard batter. The coconut will float to the top, but when the flan is turned upside down to serve, the coconut will be on the bottom.

Sautéed Mushrooms with Wine Sauce

Cogumelos ao Molho de Vinho

This rich side dish, made with plenty of wine, butter, and garlic, has been on the menu for many years. It is a perfect accompaniment for steak. You can adapt the recipe by using different types of mushrooms—wild varieties are especially good.

SERVES 4

1 lb (450 g) small or medium white mushrooms

½ cup (1 stick/115 g) butter

2 tablespoons minced garlic

1 teaspoon cracked black pepper

3 tablespoons all-purpose flour

1 small sprig rosemary, finely chopped

½ cup (120 ml) packaged demi-glace sauce, or 3 cubes beef bouillon, dissolved in ½ cup (120 ml) hot water

1 cup (240 ml) red wine

Salt

2 cups (475 ml) hot water

Wash the mushrooms under running water. If using medium-sized mushrooms, cut them in half.

Melt the butter in a saucepan over medium heat. When the butter starts to foam, add the garlic and pepper. Cook the garlic until lightly golden but not burned. With the help of a strainer or sifter, sprinkle the flour into the pan, stirring constantly, and cook for 1 minute. Stir in the rosemary and the demi-glace. Continue cooking the mixture for 1 to 2 minutes, stirring constantly with a wooden spatula; stirring is very important since you want to form a nice glaze on the bottom of the pan without it starting to burn. When the mixture starts to stick to the bottom and becomes difficult to loosen with the spatula, add the wine and stir for 1 minute. Add the mushrooms and season with salt to taste. While the mushrooms are cooking, slowly stir in the water until the sauce thickens or reaches the desired consistency (you may not need the full 2 cups). The mushrooms are ready to serve, or they can be refrigerated for up to 3 days.

Brazilian Cheese Bread

Pão de Queijo

A wonderful culinary perk at most churrascarias is a basket of flavorful cheese bread called pão de queijo. This bread originated in Minas Gerais, a state in Brazil. Minas is the Brazilian Wisconsin, and many people call the Mineiros (the habitants of Minas) "cheese eaters" due the huge amount of cheese produced in the region. These dinner rolls were created to make good use of all that cheese. The most interesting thing about these rolls is that they are made with polvilho azedo, a fine tapioca starch that is gluten-free. The crust of these delicious rolls is golden, delicate, and thin, and the interior is elastic and almost gooey due to the huge amount of cheese used in its preparation. The cheese bread made its way from farms to churrascarias and today is an indispensable part of the dining experience, served fresh and warm to diners right after they are seated. There are many regional variations of this bread, but this simple recipe is easy to make and is always a crowd pleaser.

MAKES ABOUT 24 ROLLS

4 large eggs (preferably organic)

1½ cups (135 g) grated Parmesan

2 cups (244 g) tapioca starch (also known as tapioca flour)

1¼ cup (300 ml) whole milk

½ cup (120 ml) vegetable oil

½ tablespoon kosher salt

Preheat the oven to 375°F. Mix the eggs, cheese, tapioca starch, milk, oil, and kosher salt in a blender for about 30 seconds at medium speed until a smooth batter is formed. Coat a 24-cup mini muffin pan with non-stick cooking spray, and fill each cup to the top with batter. Bake for about 20 minutes, or until lightly golden in color and almost doubled in size. Serve warm.

You can create a variation of these rolls using almost any semi-hard or hard cheese you have in the fridge. Mix the desired amount of cheese with the Parmesan to total 1½ cups (135 g). Shredded Gruyère and Comtè are some of my favorites.

Papaya Cream
Crème de Papaia

This is the must-have dessert when dining at a churrascaria. Papayas are abundant and inexpensive in Brazil. They are usually served with breakfast, but when you visit a churrascaria, almost everyone will finish their meal with crème de papaia, a dessert that looks like a thick milkshake and is served in a goblet. This dessert is popular not only because it is extremely refreshing and delicious, but also because papaya aids in digestion—not a bad thing after consuming all that protein.

This simple dessert contains only two ingredients—ice cream and papaya—so make sure both are of high quality. Finding great papayas is the hardest part, as they are at their best when in season and are more readily available in warmer climates. The papaya should be ripe, sweet, and have a deep orange color. The ice cream should be the creamiest and richest you can find with natural vanilla flavor. When the server brings this dessert to your table at a churrascaria, he will also bring a bottle of crème de cassis and offer to pour it over the dessert. Crème de cassis is a sweet, dark liqueur made from blackcurrants. It adds a luscious finishing touch to this dessert.

SERVES 4

1 pint (500 ml) gourmet-quality vanilla ice cream

1 medium ripe papaya

Crème de cassis liqueur (optional)

Chill four 16-ounce (475 ml) goblets, parfait glasses, or other serving dishes in the freezer. Move the ice cream from the freezer to the refrigerator or kitchen counter to soften lightly, but don't let it melt. While the ice cream is softening, peel the papaya; make sure to peel deeply because the lighter-colored membrane just under the skin is bitter. After peeling, split the papaya lengthwise. Remove all of the seeds and any white membrane from the inside of the papaya with a spoon. Be very sure that all the seeds are removed; a single missed seed blended with the ice cream will turn the dessert bitter and almost inedible. Cut the papaya into small cubes and transfer to the freezer for about 5 minutes to chill; you will need 1½ cups (210 g) in total.

Add the chilled papaya and the slightly softened ice cream to an electric blender; blend at medium speed until very smooth and creamy with no lumps, about 30 seconds. If necessary, turn off the blender and use a spatula to scrape the sides and mix the ingredients; then remove the spatula and turn the blender on again. Remove the chilled goblets from the freezer and divide the papaya ice cream mixture between them. If using the crème de cassis, add a splash over the dessert before serving.

Do not mix the crème de cassis with the dessert—it tastes better when you take spoonfuls of the papaya cream and the liqueur is sitting on the side of the spoon.

The Brazilian Caipirinha

I believe there is a connection between a country's national drink, its culture, and the soul of its people. For Brazil, the caipirinha is that drink—tangy, sweet, and refreshing but potent too. An unpretentious drink, it is loved and enjoyed nationwide regardless of region, background, or income. In fact, it's a drink Brazilians love to share. At bars and restaurants, we order one caipirinha, take a sip or two, and pass it to a friend, colleague, or spouse—even a mother-in-law! When the glass is empty, we order another.

Nobody knows for sure where and how the first caipirinha originated, but one popular story is that it started out as a remedy to ease colds and the flu in the early twentieth century. It was believed that adding a small amount of a spirit, such as brandy or cachaça, to a concoction of lime juice, honey, and garlic would induce a sweat and aid in recovery. It seems likely that over time, the garlic was eliminated and the amount of cachaça increased. Since honey was not always available or affordable, it was eventually replaced with sugar, which was abundant. From there, it was just a natural evolution to add ice and create the perfect drink to endure those scalding summer days on the beach. There is certainly a fair amount of veracity to this story. I even recall Carlito, my father-in-law, quite often using the excuse that he was feeling a little "under the weather" in order to make a huge caipirinha with honey and lime juice.

There are only three ingredients in a caipirinha: cachaça, lime, and sugar. The quality of the cachaça is important but so is the quality of the lime. The best limes to use are Persian limes, but Key limes also work well. These limes will render a lot of juice with just the right tartness for the cocktail. Whether you use Persian, Key, or local limes, they should have a very thin and smooth green peel without spots. If the lime has a textured peel like thick leather, it will be dry and the juice will not be as flavorful. The limes must be cut and muddled (crushed) at the very last minute or else the juice will be bitter, ruining the caipirinha. Note that you do not use freshly squeezed lime juice to make a caipirinha; you use lime wedges that have been muddled with a muddler. Be consistent in the pressure of your muddling; otherwise, the amount of juice extracted from the limes will vary and each caipirinha may be slightly different in flavor intensity.

While many Brazilians and bartenders use cane sugar in their preparation, we prefer to use simple syrup at Texas de Brazil. But there is method in our madness: granulated sugar doesn't dissolve easily with the cachaça and lime juice, so much of it is left sitting on the bottom of the glass. To avoid this and create a more evenly blended drink, we make our own syrup using the same sugar. There is no difference in flavor between a caipirinha made with sugar versus simple syrup; the syrup is just easier to use.

The perfect caipirinha is a well-balanced drink that is not too sweet, not too strong, and not too sour—it should taste smooth, delicious, and refreshing. With a bit of practice, you'll get it just right. So buy a bottle of cachaça, grab some fresh limes and sugar, and then raise your glass and say "Saúde."

Texas de Brazil Classic Caipirinha

Caipirinhas are made with cachaça, a spirit distilled from the fresh juice of sugar cane, which is abundant and inexpensive in Brazil. Cachaça is the most popular distilled spirit in the country. It is also known as aguardente or pinga, along with hundreds of nicknames that were coined when the spirit was banned for a period in the seventeenth century and again in the eighteenth century. Cachaça is often compared with rum, which is made from molasses rather than pure sugar cane. Though this spirit dates back to the colonial era of Brazil, it has only recently been distributed to other parts of the world.

The caipirinha is not a gaucho-inspired cocktail—it first gained popularity farther north, most likely in Rio de Janeiro or Bahia. When you think of the caipirinha, you think of the beach, not the Pampas. The gauchos from the early days didn't drink caipirinhas. They would drink cachaça straight—and lots of it—but not as a cocktail with sugar and slices of lime; that would be much too fancy. But as the gaucho culture and churrasco cuisine became recognized in other parts of Brazil, the caipirinha became the perfect drink to sip while grilling churrasco, particularly during a Sunday meal. While the men were gathered around the fire grilling meats, many times the women would make caipirinhas, and they would drink together, sharing with the rest of their family and friends.

SERVES 1

1 medium Persian lime

1½ fl oz (45 ml) simple syrup (recipe on facing page)

Ice cubes

2 fl oz (60 ml) good-quality cachaça

Wash the lime and cut lengthwise into quarters. Cutting in this direction will reveal a white line, which is the pithy core. Use a paring knife to remove this core, or the caipirinha will be bitter. Cut each piece in half again to create 8 pieces in total, and place them in a short and heavy 10-ounce glass. Using a muddler, smash the lime to extract as much juice as possible. Be careful not to overdo it, or you may extract the bitter oils from the skin. Add the simple syrup and stir with a spoon. Fill the glass with ice cubes (not nugget, crushed, or flaked ice) and pour in the cachaça. Transfer the contents to a martini shaker, cover, and shake gently for only 4 to 5 seconds. Transfer the liquid and ice back to the glass and serve immediately.

Cut the lime just minutes before preparing the drink. Cut limes will oxidize upon contact with air and turn bitter.

Strawberry Caipirinha with Mint

Caipirinha de Morango e Menta

This is a fruity variation on the classic recipe. The quality of this caipirinha will depend on the quality and ripeness of the strawberries you're using, so sample the berries first to make sure they are bursting with flavor and sweetness.

SERVES 1

4 medium very ripe strawberries, sliced

2–3 mint leaves

1 fl oz (30 ml) simple syrup (recipe below)

2 fl oz (60 ml) cachaça

Ice cubes

Place the strawberries and the mint leaves in a short glass and crush with a muddler. Add the simple syrup and cachaça and stir. Fill the rest of the glass with ice cubes (not nugget, crushed, or flaked ice), leaving enough room to stir the caipirinha with a spoon. Enjoy.

Variation:
Pomegranate arils are a somewhat tart alternative to strawberries. Substitute about 2 tablespoons for the strawberries, and leave out the mint leaves.

SIMPLE SYRUP

1 cup (200 g) sugar

½ cup (120 ml) water

In a small pot, bring the sugar and water to a boil. When the water begins to simmer, mix the sugar with a spoon for about 30 seconds, then let it cook for another 2 to 3 minutes. Turn off the heat and transfer the syrup to a heatproof container. Let the syrup cool, then place the container in the refrigerator. The simple syrup can be refrigerated for up to 2 months and used to make about 15 caipirinhas.

Pomegranate Caipirinha

BRAZILIAN GLOSSARY AND PRONUNCIATION GUIDE

acarajé (ah-cah-rah-ZHAY)—falafel-like balls made of black-eyed peas and onions

adaga (a-DA-ga)—dagger-type knife carried on the belt of gauchos, often used to cut meat

alho (A-leeo)—garlic

arroz (ah-ROZ)—rice

assada (ah-SAH-da)—roast

azeite (ah-ZAY-tee)—oil

bacalhau (bock-AL-yow)—dried and salted cod

batata (ba-TA-ta)—potato

batida (ba-CHEE-da)—a blended drink or cocktail made with fruit juice and liquor

bolinho (bol-EEN-yo)—scone or dumpling

bomba (BOAM-ba)—metal straw used for sipping yerba mate

bombacha (bom-BAH-sha)—baggy trousers

botequim (bo-ta-KEEN)—tavern

brigadeiro (bri-ga-DAY-ro)—a chocolate confection, similar to a truffle, that is round and covered with chocolate sprinkles

cachaça (ka-SHA-sa)—Brazilian alcoholic beverage distilled from sugar cane

caipirinha (kay-pee-REEN-ya)—Brazil's national drink made of cachaça, muddled lime, sugar, and ice

caldo de res (KAL-do dee RES)—beef broth or stock

camarão (kahm-a-RAUN)—shrimp

campeiro (kahm-PEY-ro)—Pampas

carne (KAR-nay)—meat (generally beef)

carneiro (kar-NEY-ro)—lamb (see *ovelha*)

carne seca (KAR-nay SAY-ka)—beef jerky

carniceria (carn-nay-say-REEA)—Latin butcher shop

carreteiro (KA-re-TAIR-ro)—wagoner rice

carvão (car-VAUN)—charcoal

cavaquinho (ka-va-KEEN-yo)—small guitar

cerveja (sir-VAY-zha)—beer

charque (SHAR-kay)—salted and cured meat

chimarrão (she-ma-HAUN)—yerba mate beverage

churrascaria (shoo-ras-ka-REEYA)—a Brazilian steakhouse restaurant that serves authentic churrasco-style cuisine

churrasco (shoo-RAS-ko)—Brazilian-style barbecue

churrasqueira (shoo-ras-KAY-rah)—a barbeque grill used in churrasco cooking

coco (KO-ko)—coconut

codorna (ko-DOR-nah)—quail

coração de frango (co-RA-saun dee FRAN-go) —chicken hearts

costela gorda (kos-TE-la GOR-da)—large, fat ribs

couve (KOU-vee)—kale or collard greens

coxinha (ko-SHEEN-yah)—chicken croquette shaped like a drumstick

cren (krin)—horseradish

cuia (KOO-yah)—gourd

disco de arado (DIS-ko duh ah-RAD-oh)—plow disc

dendê (den-DAY)—oil from the dendê palm tree

doce (DOH-see)—dessert or sweets

empada (aim-PA-da)—a baked half-moon-shaped pastry stuffed with meat, cheese, or vegetables

espinafre (ees-pin-AH-free)—spinach

farinha (fa-REEN-ya)—starch or flour made from ground manioc (cassava) root

farofa (fa-RO-fa)—a Brazilian side dish made of roasted farinha, oil or butter, and/or vegetables

feijão (fay-JAUN)—beans

feijoada (fay-jo-WA-da)—a popular Brazilian stew of black beans with meat, pork, and sausages

frango (FRANG-oh)—chicken

galinha (ga-LEEN-ya)—chicken stew

gaúcho (ga-OO-sho)—a native of the Rio Grande do Sul (southern) region of Brazil

Havainas (ha-va-YAN-as)—a brand of flip-flop sandals (also the Brazilian word for Hawaiians)

leite (LAY-che)—milk

linguiça (lin-GWEE-sa)—Portuguese pork sausage

lombinho (lom-BEEN-yo)—tenderloin

mandioca (mahn-gee-O-ka)—a root vegetable native to Brazil (also known as manioc, cassava, or yucca)

matambre (MA-tam-bray)—a type of flank steak rolled and stuffed with vegetables, cooked eggs, and cheese

molho (MOHL-yo)—a Brazilian sauce similar to salsa

moqueca (moh-KE-kah)—fish stew made of coconut milk and various seafood and/or fish

moranga (mo-RANG-ah)—squash

morango (mo-RANG-oh)—strawberry

ovelha (oh-VAIL-ya)—lamb or sheep

palmito (pal-MEE-toh)—hearts of palm

pão de queijo (paun de KAY-sho)—Brazilian cheese rolls

passadores (pah-sah-DOOR-es)—servers at a churrascaria

pastel (pas-TELL)—a fried half-moon-shaped pastry stuffed with sweet and savory fillings

peixe (pay-SHEE)—fish

picanha (pee-CON-ya)—a popular beef cut used in churrasco (similar to sirloin cap)

pilcha (PILL-sha)—traditional gaucho costumes

pimenta malagueta (pee-MEN-ta MAL-a-get-a)—a small, hot, red Brazilian bell pepper

porco (POR-ko)—pork

polvilho (po-VEEL-yo)—powder or starch

polvilho azedo (po-VEEL-yo a-ZED-do)—tapioca starch

queijo (KAY-sho)—cheese

quindim (KIN-jeem)—coconut flan

rodizio (ro-DEE-zee-oh)—rotation-style dining that offers a variety of grilled meats served tableside

salgadinhos (sal-ga-JEE-nhos)—tapas-like snacks

sal grosso (sal GRO-so)—course salt

salpicão (sal-pee-CAUN)—salad

saúde (saw-OOD-dee)—a toast "to your health"

sobrecoxa (so-bray-CO-sha)—chicken drumstick

toicinho (toy-SEEN-oh)—bacon

torresmo (TOR-res-mo)—pig crackling

tropeiro (tro-PAIR-ro)—cattleman

INDEX

Metric Conversion Chart

VOLUME MEASUREMENTS		WEIGHT MEASUREMENTS		TEMPERATURE CONVERSION	
U.S.	Metric	U.S.	Metric	Fahrenheit	Celsius
1 teaspoon	5 ml	½ ounce	15 g	250	120
1 tablespoon	15 ml	1 ounce	30 g	300	150
¼ cup	60 ml	3 ounces	90 g	325	160
⅓ cup	75 ml	4 ounces	115 g	350	180
½ cup	125 ml	8 ounces	225 g	375	190
⅔ cup	150 ml	12 ounces	350 g	400	200
¾ cup	175 ml	1 pound	450 g	425	220
1 cup	250 ml	2 ¼ pounds	1 kg	450	230

ACKNOWLEDGMENTS

Many thanks to all the people who helped me with this book, especially June Rifkin Clark, for always looking for the right words and constantly reminding me about the deadlines; my agent, Stephany Evans, at FinePrint Literary Management; my editor, Madge Baird, and the team at Gibbs Smith; Robbie Robertson, who taught me so much about beef; Leonardo Pierret, for helping me with all the cooking and plating; and Denny Culbert, for the great photos. Additionally, I want to thank Hannah, Candyce, Josuel, Lucas, Fabio, Willie, and many others I've worked with over the years.